Three Minutes a Day

VOLUME 45

THREE MINUTES A DAY
VOLUME 45

Mary Ellen Robinson
Vice President

Stephanie Raha
Editor-in-Chief

The Christophers
5 Hanover Square, 11th Floor
New York, NY 10004

www.christophers.org

O God, You are my God,

I seek You,

my soul thirsts for You. ...

Because Your steadfast love is better than life,

my lips will praise You.

So I will bless You as long as I live;

I will lift my hands and call on Your name. ...

For You have been my help,

and in the shadow of Your wings I sing for joy.

my soul clings to You;

Your right hand upholds me.

PSALM 63

The Christophers warmly thank
all our friends, sponsors and supporters
who have made this 45th volume of
Three Minutes a Day possible.

We offer our special appreciation
to the following for their
contributions to this book:

Joan Bromfield

John DiChiaro

Monica Ann Yehle Glick

Margaret O'Connell

Karen Hazel Radenbaugh

Jill Wronski

Iris Zalun

Introduction

Warmest greetings and God's blessings as you enjoy this edition of *Three Minutes a Day!* The Christophers' founder, Maryknoll Father James Keller, believed that every person is born with a God-given purpose and has a responsibility to be "an active participant in life rather than a passive onlooker." His goal for these books was to share daily inspiration, to draw you closer to God, and to motivate you to make a positive difference. That remains the goal for this 45th volume...and the goal for all Christopher work.

Please know that we appreciate your ongoing Christopher support. Because of your help, we continue Father Keller's mission of spreading God's love, light and hope to a world in need through Christopher News Notes, the *Christopher Closeup* radio show and podcast, the Christopher Awards, Christopher Leadership Courses for Adults and Teens, and more. We also donate our books and News Notes to prison ministries and to our military men and women overseas who value our encouraging materials.

You, dear friend, are the reason we are able to light so many candles of hope and to inspire others to do the same. God bless you always.

Mary Ellen Robinson
Vice President
The Christophers

An Answer to Your Prayer

Does it sometimes seem as though God is not listening to your prayers? Writer Anthony DeStefano suggests that you pray for things God will never deny you. The author of *Ten Prayers God Always Says Yes To: Divine Answers to Life's Most Difficult Problems* asks you to consider these prayers to start:

"Forgive me." As long as you admit your faults and try to make amends, God will always give you another chance.

"Give me courage." Whatever our fears, God will give us the courage we lack to do what's right.

"Get me through this!" Sometimes it takes longer than we want to work our way through tough times, but God will take care of us—if we keep our trust in Him.

As long as you open yourself to His will, God will always be with you—and always say "Yes!"

Pray in the Spirit at all times in every prayer and supplication. (Ephesians 6:18)

Eternal God, hold my hand as I make my way through life.

The Hope Within

Father Peter LeJacq is a physician and Maryknoll Missioner who runs a hospital in Tanzania. One day, during the Rwanda genocide, he saw a refugee woman approaching the hospital. When Father LeJacq reached her, she collapsed in his arms.

The woman told the priest that she had been forced to watch her husband and children hacked to death, and that she was then raped. After some time, the missionary gently asked her if she had lost her faith because of her sufferings and loss.

But she answered, "Oh no, Father! You see, there is God in me, and there is God in you, and if there is God in you, there is hope in you."

Think about your life and your faith. Think about God in you and in all of us.

Why are you cast down, O my soul? ...Hope in God; for I shall again praise him, my help and my God. (Psalm 43:5)

Blessed Trinity, help me strive to show my love for You by loving my neighbor.

A Woman's Touch

Recent studies show that women now surpass men in the field of philanthropic giving. This may be a reflection of the gains women are making in earning power, wealth and financial control.

Pamela Fiori, editor-in-chief of *Town & Country* magazine, feels that women participate in charities more when someone close to them is stricken with a sickness or injury. According to Fiori, a personal experience "makes them realize they can do more than empathize."

Women also volunteer in many different areas. Some participate in environmental causes, while others lend their assistance in the fields of medicine and social work. Those who volunteer their time as well as their money to charity are true role models.

Sacrificing our time and abundance to help others is a good step to lead someone closer to God.

Each of you must give as you have made up your mind, not reluctantly or under compulsion. (2 Corinthians 9:7)

Lord, lend me the strength to help those who are in need.

Cold Feet

There is nothing more exhilarating than experiencing the beauty of nature first-hand.

Ice climbing is a sport which requires physical and mental training. One must prepare to overcome the bitter cold.

Matt Shove has been an ice climbing guide in New England for years. His job is to lead people through the basic techniques. He teaches his students how to walk on horizontal and vertical surfaces wearing crampons, or shoes with spikes that allow people to move along icy surfaces, including frozen waterfalls.

Most students find the sport daunting, but physically and mentally refreshing.

Throughout life, we are going to encounter many obstacles. We must train our minds and reach out to God so that He can help us embrace the beauty in the world.

Train yourself in godliness, for, while physical training is of some value, godliness is valuable in every way. (1 Timothy 4:7)

Paraclete, bless us with strength and wisdom.

Your Local Library — Check It Out

Libraries hold a world of promise, not just the latest bestsellers and children's videos.

Women's Day magazine featured people who found hope and healing at these community fixtures. Elaine Elinson, 61, took a break from her hospital vigil during her husband's serious illness. Drawn to the "familiar golden glow of the lights illuminating the books" at a San Francisco library, she found the comfort of Mary Oliver's poetry.

Amy Smith, 33, of Minneapolis had suffered two miscarriages. When she finally gave birth, she was surprised and troubled to find that she had postpartum depression. Researching the condition at her library, she came upon Brooke Shields' compelling story. If a star could cope, she felt, so could she.

A library can be a great blessing in tough times. Enjoy and support your local branch.

Here I am; in the scroll of the book it is written of me. I delight to do your will, O my God. (Psalm 40:7-8)

Savior, show me how to use the wisdom of others well.

Becoming Clutter-Free

In his book *Enough Already!* Peter Walsh offers his prescription for a clutter-free life, including your inner life. "The first step toward clearing the clutter of your internal life—what I call spiritual clutter—is to clarify to yourself what your goals are." He suggests these general goals:

- **A sense of purpose or mission.** What are your core beliefs?

- **A sense of completion.** Do you need more time to meditate and feel centered?

- **Community.** What is your place in the world?

- **Decompression.** What do you do to relax and regroup?

- **Charity.** Do you clear physical and mental clutter by giving of yourself to others?

Try to strike a balance in your life. Get rid of unnecessary things and cherish things of true value.

The kingdom of heaven is like a net that was thrown into the sea. ...When it was full, they drew it ashore...and put the good into baskets but threw out the bad. (Matthew 13: 47-48)

Guide me, Holy Spirit, in my choices.

Protecting Irreplaceable Treasures

In the midst of the Second World War's destructiveness, a small group of American and British soldiers salvaged much of the West's cultural history, according to Ilaria Dagnini Brey's book *The Venus Fixers: The Remarkable Story of the Allied Soldiers Who Saved Italy's Art During World War II.*

These soldiers, mostly architects, artists and art historians, risked their lives to protect or repair churches, palaces, libraries, the great paintings of the Uffizi, and other treasures.

General Dwight Eisenhower authorized the team to conduct this mission. "Today we are fighting in a country which has contributed a great deal to our cultural inheritance," he said, "a country which by their creation helped...the growth of civilization which is ours. We are bound to respect those monuments so far as war allows."

It's important to preserve precious and irreplaceable treasures—those made by man and those made by God.

You are a hiding place for me; You preserve me from trouble. (Psalm 32:7)

May I celebrate all that is good and beautiful, Father.

Release Your Resentment

It's been said that holding on to resentment is like drinking poison and expecting the other person to die.

Michael Josephson, ethicist and founder of the Character Count! project, believes that "grudges are nothing more than toxic memories of how someone made us feel."

He continues, "Perhaps we fool ourselves into thinking we can inflict some sort of pain on the person who wronged us. It doesn't matter how justified the bitter feelings are or how right we are. Holding on to a grievance turns pain into suffering. In a peculiar way, it empowers the wrongdoer to hurt us again and again.

"Give yourself a great gift. Let go of your grudges so you can move forward and free yourself of the chains of resentment."

If you're holding on to a grudge, let it go. It will change your life for the better.

I will forgive their inequity, and remember their sin no more. (Jeremiah 31:34)

Christ, You died for our sins. Help us to forgive one another as You forgive us.

99 and Joyful

Sarah Gellert, aged 99 and counting, lives alone with almost no savings, impaired hearing, vision and mobility and few surviving, close-by family members.

One of ten siblings, she was the only one to survive childhood. She has been twice widowed and has outlived friends as well as former co-workers from her career in a Manhattan financial firm. Still, she has stepdaughters, a granddaughter, and a brother-in-law as well as a friend from kindergarten.

Gellert paid for her own 24-hour home care until her savings were exhausted. Then the Jewish Association for Services for the Aged helped her apply for Medicaid and food stamps.

The almost-centenarian says, "When you make a friend, you have one for life" and "that I'm here is a miracle." She adds, "It's not my temperament to complain."

Just being alive is good. Work on being positive.

A joyful heart is life itself. (Sirach 30:22)

Support our efforts to be thankful and positive, God.

"Walking" Buses

Elementary schools in Lecco, Italy, have found a way to combat childhood obesity, traffic jams and a rise in greenhouse gases. Each morning, about 450 students travel along 17 school-bus routes—on foot.

More than half the students at the Carducci School take the "walking bus," or *piedibus*, (foot-bus in Italian). Each morning, staff members and parent volunteers lead lines of walking students to school, stopping here and there to pick up more children along the way.

Many of them were previously driven to school. Although the *piedibus* routes are generally less than one mile, the new system has eliminated more than 100,000 miles of car travel and thousands of tons of greenhouse gases. In addition, the children are walking up to a mile a day—a definite health benefit.

Adults can inspire children. Start walking and encourage family and friends to do the same.

**Leave to the young a noble example.
(2 Maccabees 6:28)**

Help adults set children a healthy and "green" example, Creation's Lord.

With Respect and Harmony

James Krenov was not merely a famed cabinetmaker whose aesthetic prowess influenced a generation of furniture makers through his clean, integrated and delicate designs.

Krenov also wrote tirelessly on his craft and became as well known for his philosophy of furniture design and cabinetry as he was for his creations themselves. He founded the influential woodworking program at the College of the Redwoods in Fort Bragg, California.

The cabinetmaker once wrote, "Let us know our wood as we do our hands, and work with it in common respect and harmony." When he died in 2009, he was holding a piece of sandalwood that he had shaped and smoothed, a final sign of his passion for his work.

Choose to do your job with passion and excellence.

A skilled woodcutter may...with pleasing workmanship make a useful vessel. (Wisdom of Solomon 13:11)

Infuse me with enthusiasm for my life, Gentle Savior.

In Her Memory

Michelle Moglia and Mia Walters were best friends. Walters and her family moved to Australia when the girls were in the fourth grade, but they kept in touch over the next few years through letters and the Internet. When Moglia learned that her friend had been diagnosed with cancer, she was distraught. "I really wished I was there for her during her sickness," she says.

Mia Walters died from cancer at 16. Two days later, Michelle Moglia founded Forever Friends to memorialize Walters, to raise money for cancer research and to comfort patients by distributing teddy bears. She's already held a community Walk-a-thon for the cause.

Cherish your friends while they are still with you and, since death is but a temporary separation, after they have died.

I know that my Redeemer lives and that...after my skin has been thus destroyed, then in my flesh I shall see God. (Job 19:25,26)

Strengthen our belief that friendships are only temporarily interrupted by death, Eternal God.

Making Music for Monkeys

Music can alter our emotions; make us happy or sad; soothed or excited. But how? One composer says he found the answer by writing music for monkeys!

David Teie has played cello with the National Symphony Orchestra and with Metallica. He feels music stirs us because it relates to the most primitive sounds we make and respond to—laughter, heartbeats, a mother's cooing, for example.

He recorded the sounds monkeys create when they are mellow, happy, frightened and angry. Then he composed music to match those sounds. These musical compositions evoked the same emotions in the monkeys as the natural sounds they mirrored.

Everyday sights and sounds influence how we think and feel. But always we should strive to hold onto the joy that comes from knowing God's love for us.

I have put my hope in the Everlasting...and joy has come to me from the Holy One. (Baruch 4:22)

Make firm my hope in You, Lord. Fill me with Your joy.

Do You Want to Be Nicer?

A study by the University of Rochester (NY) found that nature actually makes us nicer.

"The health benefits of nature range from more rapid healing to stress reduction to improved mental performance and vitality," says Richard Ryan, professor of psychology and co-author of the study.

But what do you do when winter comes and you spend more time indoors, especially in your office? Try these remedies:

Keep a hardy philodendron in a colorful pot. Use a nature-themed mouse pad, calendar and screen saver. Listen to nature sounds on CDs. Tack up favorite nature and animal photos.

"It's about stopping and smelling the roses as opposed to passing them by while you think of your next meeting," adds Ryan.

Appreciate God's creation wherever you are.

The Lord God took the man and put him in the garden of Eden to till it and to keep it. (Genesis 2:15)

Remind us to seek Your peace in communion with Your Creation, Generous Father.

Haircuts and Hope

Cristiano Cora placed an unusual ad for his hair salon. Instead of his standard $100 and up haircuts, he offered free haircuts to anyone who showed up one Saturday—with proof of unemployment.

Theresa Cheung, an out-of-work fashion designer, had trimmed expenses including her usual hair cuts during her four months' unemployment. But to find a job she needed to look as though she "had little to worry about."

Carmen Ramirez, a former fashion buyer learning medical billing, also took Cora's offer. "This is starting the change," she said.

Cora, his staff and other stylists, were trying to help people get jobs by helping them keep up their appearances. In return, they hoped their own business would improve in the long-run.

When being generous, remember that both the one giving and the one receiving benefit.

The measure you give will be the measure you get, and still more will be given you. (Mark 4:24)

Remind us to be big-hearted and open-handed, Lord.

"A Midwinter Night's Dream"

After two Northport, New York, teachers were diagnosed with Lou Gehrig's disease (Amyotrophic Lateral Sclerosis or ALS) in 2004, students staged a charity basketball tournament. They raised $32,000 and donated it to Johns Hopkins University's ALS research center.

When Harold Garrecht, president of a brokerage firm, heard about their efforts, he wrote a check and then offered to show the students how professionals raise money for charities.

His efforts worked. The young people held their first Midwinter Night's Dream gala the following year. They put the whole event together, designing invitations, sending out press releases and even serving as waiters. And in the years since they have raised over $1,000,000 for ALS research. The group has changed as some students graduate and others take their places, but the good work continues.

What an inspiring achievement for high school kids!

Set an example. (Judith 8:24)

Remind adults that teens and children can set a good example, Jesus.

The Best First Sergeant

Command Sgt. Maj. Teresa L. King is the first woman to run one of the Army's tough schools for drill instructors.

The eighth of 12 children, King is the daughter of a sharecropper who grew cucumbers and tobacco near Fort Bragg, North Carolina. Now, at Fort Jackson, South Carolina, she will influence the basic training of enlisted soldiers for years to come by overseeing the drill instructors who guide them.

Rising to the top in the armed forces has not been easy for Sgt. Maj. King. One of only five women in her drill-sergeant school graduating class, she was promoted despite objections from some who believed the job belonged to a man.

"Turns out she was the best first sergeant they ever had," said one retired supervisor.

Prejudice benefits no one. Erase it from your mind and your heart.

With the judgment you make you will be judged. (Matthew 7:2)

Deliver us from the evil of prejudice, Father God.

Better Living — Through Plumbing?

A recent Gallup survey published in *The Wall Street Journal* showed that business owners — plumbers, gardeners, and the like — ranked higher in personal satisfaction and well-being than those who work for others. What explains business owners' relative happiness?

According to Roger Peugeot, owner of a 14-employee plumbing firm in Overland Park, Kansas, autonomy over his work, a connection and presence in his community, and personal relationships with his employees, customers and suppliers are among the reasons for his satisfaction.

"I'm still excited to get up and go to work every day," says Peugeot.

There's a lot to be said for taking responsibility for your own work and life. Consider how you can increase your own well-being in life.

Wisdom is as good as an inheritance, an advantage to those who see the sun. ...The advantage of knowledge is that wisdom gives life to the one who possesses it. (Ecclesiastes 7:11-12)

Abide with us, Spirit of Wisdom.

Making Smart Choices

Known by many as America's "favorite cheapskate," writer Mary Hunt has advised many people on ways to stretch what seems to be a perpetually shrinking dollar.

In tough economic times, Hunt suggests the following ways to eke more bang out of every buck:

Keep a written record of all your expenditures. It's surprising to see exactly where your money is going.

Consider your retirement funds sacrosanct. It's tempting to tap into retirement money for living expenses, but risky to your long-term financial health.

Give to God. This demonstrates faith in His promise to supply all of our needs.

And don't be afraid to reconsider your priorities and those of your family. Decide what's really most important.

Cast all your anxiety on (God), because He cares for you. (1 Peter 5:7)

Keep me hopeful in times of struggle, Holy Spirit.

Tree of Hope

During the Holocaust in the Theresienstadt concentration camp, in what is now the Czech Republic, Irma Lauscher wanted to celebrate Tu Bishvat, the Jewish "New Year of the Trees." She convinced a workman to bring her a sapling in his boot. Child prisoners sacrificed some of their water rations to keep it alive.

Lauscher survived the Holocaust. When she told authorities about the sapling which had grown into a fine sycamore tree, they transferred it to the front of the camp to memorialize those who had been murdered at Theresienstadt.

Now, 600 trees planted throughout the world come from that one tree of hope in Theresienstadt. And each tree inspires hope and peace.

Have hope despite your struggles and share it with others.

There is hope for a tree, if it is cut down, that it will sprout again. (Job 14:7)

Let me sink my roots deep into Your river of grace, God.

Start with the Basics

"Easy Ed" Macauley, a celebrated player with the Boston Celtics in the 1950's and a member of the NBA's Hall of Fame went on to become a Catholic Deacon and the author of the book, *Homilies Alive*. Here's what he wrote about the importance of mastering fundamentals as the basis of success:

"Learning the fundamentals one at a time requires intelligent practice, self-evaluation, and if available, outside advice. Success doesn't come overnight. The great players are willing to spend the hours needed practicing on the playground, in the gym, during the off-season. He or she doesn't have the time to master the fundamentals while learning the plays, the offense, the defense, and preparing for games. And so constant practice is required, but it must be intelligent practice. If the proper fundamentals are not pursued, the athlete will be practicing mistakes."

Whatever your goals, make sure you have a solid foundation.

God's firm foundation stands. (2 Timothy 2:19)

Almighty Creator, teach me how to build a solid life.

Inspiration in a Traffic Jam

As Randy Harris crawled along a Florida roadway, stuck in heavy traffic, he noticed a specialty license plate on the car just inches ahead of him that promoted wildlife conservation. He decided right there to create a plate that would promote life.

Harris founded Choose Life, Inc., an all-volunteer nonprofit organization that helps citizens make and distribute specialty license plates promoting adoption as an alternative to abortion. Money raised through the license plate program goes to safe havens, pregnancy-help centers and other agencies that provide screening, counseling, financial support and housing for pregnant women.

A decade later, 24 states have approved a "Choose Life" license plate. Eventually, Harris would like the plate to be an option in every state.

Sometimes inspiration for good comes from the most unlikely source. But how wonderful when we spot the spark to make a change!

Let everything that breathes praise the Lord! (Psalm 150:6)

May all I do, Father, give honor to Your gift of life.

Take A Closer Look

It's true that Bruno Lacorazza sells hats that seem the same, but if you look closely, and his customers do, you'll begin to see differences.

Lacorazza is a Colombian-born hatter to the Lubavitch Hasidim and other Orthodox Jews who keep their heads covered as a sign of respect for God. He's one of the country's largest suppliers of black hats to Jewish men, selling thousands annually.

While all the hats have black brims, crown, band and bow, the hatter creates different textures and dimensions for the homburgs, fedoras and other styles. So while the hats are similar at first glance, they have noticeable differences if you take a closer look.

Slow down a bit and take the time to notice the small, yet significant, things in life.

David went up the ascent of the Mount of Olives...with his head covered and walking barefoot. (2 Samuel 15:30)

The little things of life do matter, Divine Master. Teach me to understand that.

When It Seemed All Hope Was Gone

Just before Christmas a number of years ago, Sherry Canfarelli's life changed profoundly. Her husband said their marriage was over. Canfarelli wondered how she and the children would weather the holidays.

A couple from the Ginghamsville United Methodist Church in Ohio "adopted" Canfarelli and her children. They brought food, Christmas presents and comfort.

That January after the divorce papers were filed, she lost her job and the family was soon evicted. Two of her three youngsters desperately needed counseling.

Canfarelli was welcomed into the church's Bible study and encouragement group. A parishioner found her housing; another a counselor. The church's food pantry provided food.

Today, Canfarelli credits the church members, saying, "they held me" as she pulled her life together. How can you and your faith community uphold those in need of support?

As the body without the spirit is dead, so faith without works is also dead. (James 2:26)

Encourage faith communities to reach out to the troubled, to succor the aged and the ill, to guide youth, Lord.

Going Beyond Fear

When Marissa Jaret Winokur was 27, she was living her dream: she was rehearsing for her leading role in a Broadway musical. Then, out of the blue, Winokur learned she had cervical cancer. "I remember feeling like I was in a vacuum," she says of that awful moment of discovery.

But Winokur aggressively managed her own health, went onstage on opening night of her Broadway show, *Hairspray,* and soon married.

Today, Winokur no longer has cancer.

"Right now I want to do everything—I don't want the world to go by me. I want to be part of it all," she says.

In adversity, there is an opportunity for optimism and strength. Encourage those who suffer to see the light at the end of the tunnel.

May (you) abound in hope by the power of the Holy Spirit. (Romans 15:13)

Enlighten us with optimism, Savior.

Building Peace

On a trip to Jordan, Noah Baker Merrill met with a number of refugees from Iraq. Listening to their stories of pain and loss, he was overwhelmed with rage and anguish.

One of Merrill's Iraqi friends advised him not to stew in his own negativity: "I understand how you're feeling and I appreciate it. What we need from you is not to be angry and sad, but for you to work hard and stay with us."

Inspired, Merrill soon co-founded Direct Aid Iraq to provide emergency medical care and to advocate for resettlement of Iraqis affected by war. The group also attempts to build peaceful relationships between Iraqis and Americans.

Overcome your anger. Channel it into a positive project.

Anger does not produce God's righteousness. (James 1:20)

When situations anger me, Almighty God, help me find a positive outlet so that I can actually make things better, not worse.

Three Princesses at a Train Station

Weary passengers made their way off a packed commuter train one weekday evening. For many, the trials and traumas of the workday were etched in tired eyes and a slow pace.

Suddenly three little girls, each dressed as a fairy tale princess, wandered through the crowd. As they passed through, smiling faces followed them. In fact, the mood of the crowd seemed uplifted. By the time the three "princesses" reached their destination—their father, a worn-out commuter himself—and offered him joy-filled hugs, there seemed not to be a frown or furrowed brow in sight.

Joy is all around us, waiting for us to recognize and embrace it to refresh the soul and lighten life's load.

A joyful heart is life itself, and rejoicing lengthens one's life span. (Sirach 30:22)

Your love in my life, Father, brings me joy.

Join the Club

John Benish, Jr. is chief operating officer of Cook Illinois Corporation, the largest family-owned school bus company in the nation. Several years ago, he learned that kids who are regularly exposed to diesel fumes have higher risks of cancer and respiratory problems. As a result, he replaced the gas in almost all of his 2,000 buses with biodiesel fuel made from soybean oil.

Feeling that his work was unfinished, Benish also formed the Clean Air Club to encourage people to be more proactive in recycling and in protecting the environment. He created the Clean Air Club Bus, too, an interactive museum on wheels which visits schools to educate children about environmental issues.

Teach others, especially children, the importance of taking care of Earth's environment.

Train children in the right way, and when old they will not stray. (Proverbs 22:6)

Holy Spirit, help us encourage children and others through our example to care for this earth.

Remedies for Northern Winters

Short days. Bare gray trees. Bone-chilling winds. Pewter skies. Rime and hoar frost. Snow. Ice. It's time to create warmth, cheer and coziness in your home!

Drape brightly colored and patterned throws on chairs and on beds. Keep blinds and curtains open by day, closed at night (it'll be warmer, too). Keep the lights on and the heat as comfy as possible.

Use colorful velour, wool and fleece hats, scarves and sweaters.

Nurture African violets, Christmas cacti, or amaryllis which will produce beautiful flowers during the winter months.

Start a new hobby, such as sketching or scrapbooking. Start planning your spring garden or your summer vacation.

Try to do something kind for someone else. That has a way of really warming your heart.

He pours frost over the earth like salt, and icicles form like pointed thorns. The cold north wind blows, and ice freezes on the water. (Sirach 43:19-20)

Help us enjoy winter's inward-looking quality, Lord.

Meeting Grief with Hand-Sewn Love

When Clarisse Good of Lafayette, Indiana, first heard about a group of women who handmade clothing for sick babies, she had been seeking for a way to get involved.

Good felt a connection to the work done by members of Threads of Love, a national ecumenical ministry founded in 1993 to help parents of sick, premature or stillborn infants. That's because Good herself had a son who lived only six days, and she liked the idea of offering comfort to others experiencing the grief she herself felt.

Members meet regularly to fellowship as they sew, knit or crochet tiny outfits and blankets. They even create gowns for babies who don't survive to be buried in. One member calls the project one that "anyone—whether you sew well or not—can do."

How can you comfort worried or grieving parents?

Blessed are those who mourn, for they will be comforted. (Matthew 5:4)

Inspire us to comfort parents of sick or deceased infants and children, Merciful Savior.

Beating the Homework Blues

Young people aren't the only ones who may find themselves hating homework. Often, their parents join them.

"Parents, especially those who work outside the home, dread all the homework and pressure that the school year brings," says Jamie Woolf, in *Mom-in-Chief: How Wisdom from the Workplace Can Save Your Family From Chaos*. She recommends these strategies for homework success.

- **Agree on goals** like no television or play time until homework's done.

- **Provide a study area** free from distractions.

- **Assess your children.** Are they struggling because they don't want to do homework, or because they don't understand it?

- **Don't give up if battles and bad habits resume—** reward success.

Every task deserves the fullest measure of our God-given gifts and talents.

Human success is in the hand of the Lord. (Sirach 10:5)

Remind me, Master, that with You, all things are possible.

Sitting, They Took a Stand

On February 1, 1960, four brave college students helped rewrite U.S. history—all because of where they sat in a diner.

The event took place near Greensboro, North Carolina, at a time of severe racial divisions in America. Four young men from the nearby state Agricultural & Technical College staged a lunch-counter "sit-in" that helped end racial segregation. Today, the International Civil Rights Center & Museum recognizes their courage, through a display that depicts a restored version of the very lunch counter area where the "Greensboro Four" sat down more than 50 years ago to take a stand.

What causes ignite courage and passion in you? Even a small effort can help bring change. Think about how much better the world could be with your time, talent and energy devoted to a vital cause!

Thus says the Lord: Maintain justice, and do what is right, for soon My salvation will come, and My deliverance be revealed. (Isaiah 56:1)

Embolden us, Father, with the courage to fight injustice.

Dealing with "Stuff"

STUFF!!! We have so much that we rent self-storage units, and cram attics and basements with unusable, misplaced, or seasonal items we can't seem to live without. But why do we do it?

Some of us are convinced we will be thin again—someday. Meanwhile, the too-small clothes take up valuable closet, shelf and drawer space.

Others of us buy too many "bargains." Good deals are fine—if you write a list of what you need and keep to it—and if you have clean, accessible storage space.

Then there are those of us who love holidays. There isn't a holiday for which we don't adorn every room, assuming we can find the decorations we put away. If we can't find them, we purchase new ones!

Try sharing your usable but unused extra stuff with those who really need it.

Whoever has two coats must share with anyone who has none. (Luke 3:11)

Jesus, help us be content with enough and with an uncluttered life.

Pet Social Worker

Ed Sayres's father was the trainer for a prominent dog fancier, so it's only natural that his first word was "doggie." As he grew older, he helped his father feed and groom dogs.

Then Sayres changed direction. He earned a master's degree in psychology and worked with at-risk teens. That's when his father asked him to set up a children's educational program at St. Hubert's Animal Welfare Center. He did—and stayed 20 years, becoming president.

After starting a no-kill shelter for the San Francisco SPCA, Ed Sayres became Chief Executive of the American Society for the Prevention of Cruelty to Animals. The Society advocates for the compassionate treatment of animals, provides legal protection and prosecutes cases of animal cruelty.

Treat animals humanely and encourage others to do the same.

God made the wild animals...the cattle...and everything that creeps...And God saw that it was good. (Genesis 1:25)

Remind us that all animals, domestic and wild, are Your creatures, Lord and Creator.

When Bad Things Happen

Sister Judy Gomila wrote notes to friends while sitting in a room at her New Orleans convent—and wearing a coat and two sweaters. The boiler in the old building had broken, and it would take a couple of days to fix it. But the heat would return, Sister Judy thought to herself, while saying a prayer for all who had no heat and little hope of its return.

Meanwhile on the east coast, Monica Glick, after reading extensively about the devastation of the earthquake in Haiti, gave her daughter and her husband extra hugs that evening after work. She vowed to show such affection more often, acknowledging the great blessing they are to her every day.

In all of life's ups and downs, it's best for each of us to keep things in perspective. Stay grateful for life and its inherent goodness.

Great is the Lord, and greatly to be praised; His greatness is unsearchable. (Psalm 145:3)

In my sorrow, You send Your joy, Lord; in my suffering, Your peace.

A Healing Belief

Most Americans look to doctors and hospitals when they are sick. But not so the Hmong people who emigrated to the U.S. after the Vietnam War.

For them, shamans play an integral part in a patient's overall treatment and healing. Says one Hmong patient, "The soul is the shaman's responsibility."

In light of the Hmong's reliance on spiritual matters in getting well, some U. S. hospitals in areas with a large Hmong population allow shamans to assist patients who so choose, in addition to traditional western medicine.

It's important to grow in knowledge and tolerance for the traditions of other cultures. Just as we want the respect of our neighbors, we need to offer the same to them.

When you are ill...pray...give up your faults... cleanse your heart...offer a sweet-smelling sacrifice...then give the physician his place. (Sirach 38:9,10,11,12)

Show us, Christ, how to live in peace and tolerance.

The Womb of Healing

New York Times reporter Dana Jennings has had surgery, radiation and hormone therapy for aggressive prostate cancer. Physically he's now well. But he's had post-treatment depression and needs time and quiet to reinterpret himself.

He said in the *Times* that he "craves homely days built around writing, reading and time spent with family and friends" in order to accept his vulnerability and enter the "womb of healing."

Jennings takes pleasure in walking his dog, getting a haircut, meeting a friend for a meal, walking, culling his possessions and "vanishing into a good novel or compact disc." He finds solitude "an agreeable pal."

Take simplicity and solitude as your companions; introduce them to sociability, too.

For God alone my soul waits in silence; from Him comes my salvation. He alone is my rock and my salvation, my fortress; I shall never be shaken. (Psalm 62:1-2)

Encourage us to balance silence with noise; stillness with activity; solitude with companionship, Jesus our Savior.

The Year of the Budget

No matter your family's economic status, it's likely that over the last couple of years you have made a conscious effort to spend less money.

Cutting back can be painful, but, according to Paula Spencer writing in *Woman's Day* magazine, the process can bring lifelong benefits. For example, spending less can mean that people will take better care of the possessions they already have.

Also, the compulsion to buy for the sake of buying can diminish. Deprivation could spark a renewed sense of ambition and bolster the work ethic. And family members can gain greater respect for the value of hard work on the part of everyone.

"It's natural to want to give our kids the moon," says Spencer. "But the tight economy reminds us of a more necessary gift: solid ground."

Give your children the gift of strong roots.

Are not five sparrows sold for two pennies? Yet not one of them is forgotten in God's sight. ...Do not be afraid; you are of more value than many sparrows. (Luke 12:6,7)

Keep me focused on what matters, Holy Spirit.

The Birds of the Air

Animals and birds. Plants and flowers. Earth and sky and weather. Can we learn from nature? Jesus did. He often referred to creation: "consider the lilies, how they grow"…"as a hen gathers her brood under her wings"…and "when you see a cloud rising in the west" are just three instances.

So too the poet Walt Whitman, who wrote: "I think I could turn and live with animals, they are so placid and self-contain'd …Not one is dissatisfied, not one is demented with the mania of owning things,…Not one is respectable or unhappy over the whole earth."

Worship, live, love, laugh, work. Value people and your self over things and status. Be content with a sufficiency. And appreciate all God's creation, all God's creatures.

Strive first for the kingdom of God and His righteousness. …Do not worry about tomorrow. (Matthew 6:33,34)

Open our eyes to the life lessons Your Creation wants to teach us, Lord of life.

A Cold Awakening

The L Street Brownies of Boston calls itself the oldest polar bear club in the country. That means that the members swim in freezing water, whether an outdoor pool, a lake or the ocean. Participants often prepare by warming up in a steam bath. Next, they will go out and swim about ten to twenty strokes.

Jack Dever, the 70-year-old president of the group, grew up swimming in Dorchester Bay, and not just in the summer. While he admits that it's a shock to the system to jump into icy water in the winter, he insists that "It's addictive. You tolerate things when you swim in cold water."

Sometimes, embracing difficult conditions can help you to better appreciate life. And that may assist in facing all your problems. Whatever you do, strive to fulfill your mission in life and to develop your relationship with God.

Restore us to Yourself, O Lord.
(Lamentations 5:21)

Divine Master, grant me the strength to endure whatever hardships come my way. Guide me in caring for my neighbors in their troubles, as well.

Appearances Are Deceiving

When Lori Larsen's younger sister Kristin committed suicide at the age of 31, Larsen was overcome with grief. She recalled her childhood jealousies of her slender, popular sister.

Kristin's death also revealed a constant struggle with depression and low self-esteem—troubles Larsen never dreamed her "perfect" sister was battling. Larsen, on the other hand, battled obesity for most of her life.

After her sister's death, Lori Larsen, who weighed almost 300 pounds, decided to lose the weight that threatened her health. After she lost 100 pounds, she was finally able to ride Kristin's bicycle, a symbol of both the good health she could maintain in her sister's honor, and the pastime that her sister most enjoyed.

Appearances never tell the full story. Don't make assumptions based only on what lies on the surface.

The Lord does not see as mortals see; they look on the outward appearance, but the Lord looks on the heart. (1 Samuel 16:7)

Help us avoid snap judgments, Spirit of Love.

Life from the Bus

On one winter morning, a crowded bus crawled down New York City's Fifth Avenue. Passengers, clothed in heavy coats and packed together, almost groaned, thinking that this was no way to begin the work day.

Jenny decided instead to look outside, hoping at first just to be comforted by the promise of eventually getting off the bus. She noticed the blanket of snow that covered a large field in Central Park. She noticed dogs running and playing in another field nearby. She saw children, in colorful hats, laughing as they walked to school. She smiled as she watched moms and dads holding the hands of their little ones and walking briskly in the wintry weather.

Suddenly the bus, although still crowded, seemed to open up a bit—making room for the joy that surrounded it. Make room for joy in your life.

They shall obtain joy and gladness, and sorrow and sighing shall flee away. (Isaiah 35:10)

Thank you, Lord, for filling life with splendor to behold.

On Carefully Chosen Words

We express courtesy and kindness in so many ways. And our simplest words can encourage people, if we make the effort.

Here, as quoted in the book *Lincoln on Leadership,* is what Abraham Lincoln said about a his own efforts: "I have the popular reputation of being a story teller, but I do not deserve the name...for it is not the story itself, but its purpose, or effect, that interests me. I often avoid...a laborious explanation by a short story that illustrates my point of view. So, too, the sharpness of a refusal or the edge of a rebuke may be blunted by an appropriate story, so as to save wounded feelings and yet serve the purpose. No, I am not a simple story-teller, but story-telling as an emollient saves much friction and distress."

Choose your words with tender, loving compassion.

A word is better than a gift. (Sirach 18:16)

Enlighten me, Holy Trinity, so that I may always speak with graciousness and thoughtfulness.

Glacier National Park

Nearly a century ago, railroad baron Louis W. Hill tried to lure tourists to Montana's pristine wilderness with slogans like, "See America First." Convinced that this region was among America's most beautiful, Hill pushed Congress to establish a national park. That declaration would forever protect and preserve the jagged mountains and valleys carved out by glaciers that form what we know today as Glacier National Park.

It took years, but Hill's love of nature coupled with his enterprising business acumen helped spread awareness of the region and its unearthly beauty. Soon, even hesitant Easterners were willing to "rough it" at one of the upscale lodges Hill financed and built. And today, America's 10th national park is a thriving vacation spot.

Enjoy the beauty of the Lord's creation and do what you can to preserve His beauty and bounty.

Praise the Lord...mountains and all hills, fruit trees and all cedars! Wild animals...creeping things and flying birds! (Psalm 148:7,9-10)

Keep us open to Creation's splendor, Spirit which hovered over the waters at creation.

Ideas for the Day of Love

Valentine's Day sometimes calls for more than a box of chocolates and a store-bought card for your spouse or other loved one. Try some of these suggestions:

- Leave a special note of love and appreciation in an unexpected place, such as on the dashboard of the car, or on the kitchen table before breakfast.
- Buy his or her favorite treat, and serve it as an after-dinner surprise.
- Thank your loved one's parents for bringing such an amazing person into the world.
- Perform simple acts of kindness and respect, such as holding the door open for the other person.
- Share an umbrella in the rain.

There are many ways to say "I love you." Find creative ways to appreciate those you love.

Your love is better than wine...your name is perfume poured out. (Song of Solomon 1:2-3)

Thank you, Father God, for the people in my life, especially those closest to me.

A Much-Needed Second Chance

When Keith Swayne was released from prison in Delaware, his future looked bleak: no family members nearby; most friends lost during the two decades he had spent in prison.

That's when Paul Collins of the Society of St. Vincent de Paul Prison Ministry gave Swayne a chance for a brighter future. Collins, a 14-year volunteer in prisons, says that he's seen too many prisoners let out with nothing but "$50, a pair of shoes and nowhere to go or stay."

Says Swayne in appreciation, "I don't know what I would have done without Paul. I'd probably be back in prison."

Volunteering to help ex-convicts can help reduce the probability they will commit crimes. Thanks to the prison ministry, Swayne and others have found shelter and a job, as well as direction for a better life.

What can you do to help give someone a second chance?

I was in prison and you visited me. (Matthew 25:36)

How can we help those who have served their debt to society, Just Judge?

Achieving Dreams in a Land of Turmoil

Ramallah, West Bank, is, unfortunately, a part of the Mideast where gunshots and explosions are frequently heard.

But in 2006, Al Kamandjati (The Violinist) School opened there to rekindle interest in both Oriental and Western classical music and to teach local children how to play musical instruments. Shehade Shelaldeh, a Palestinian youth, began taking lessons there, but he switched to repairing the school's donated instruments. Learning from visiting luthiers (those who fix stringed instruments), and after a three month apprenticeship in Italy, he now has his own instrument repair shop in Ramallah.

Shelaldeh's dream "is to become a famous instrument repairer."

Like him, each of us can work hard, and share our special skills with others—even if we live in trying circumstances.

Praise the Lord with the lyre; make melody to Him with the harp of ten strings...play skillfully on the strings. (Psalm 33:2,3)

Bless musicians, artists and artisans everywhere, Eternal God.

Choosing Priorities

The cavernous brick 19th century First Baptist Church of Brattleboro, Vermont, has a 140-foot-spire. Heating the church cost $34,000 annually.

One February, the church's trustees made the Rev. Suzanne Andrews a part-time pastor and laid off the sexton. The homeless men in the church's shelter clean and vacuum, but the roof still needed repair. The congregation numbers 88 with only about 35 attending Sunday worship.

Finally, down to their last $8,000, the trustees decided to sell the 9-foot-tall, 33-inch-wide signed Tiffany window of St. John the Divine worth $60,000 to $80,000. Trustee Sylvia Seitz said that they believed "it's more important to keep the church going, even without the window."

That's a wrenching decision. But this church's priorities were in order. Are yours? And mine?

Render just decisions. (Deuteronomy 16:18)

Holy Spirit, inspire our decisions so that they are based on our heads as well as our hearts.

Blurring the Line between Black and White

Artist Alma Thomas, an African-American, was born in Georgia in 1891, yet it wasn't until 1960 that she began devoting her energies to a career that brought her critical acclaim and public recognition.

Thomas's beginnings were marked by racial violence and segregation, so her family relocated to Washington, where Thomas got a sound education and then taught art to students for 35 years. Her own painting continued, but sporadically.

Only when she retired did she begin painting full-time. She evolved into an accomplished abstract painter. When asked if she thought of herself as a black artist, she stated, "No, I do not. I'm a painter; I'm an American."

Focusing on our united strengths and commonalities can help ease racial divides. What can you do to improve race relations in your own community?

You shall love the Lord your God with all your heart. ...This is the greatest and first commandment. And the second is like it: You shall love your neighbor as yourself. (Matthew 22:37-39)

Help unite our beloved country, Prince of Peace.

"Us" and "Them"

"The only thing that makes me any different from 'those homeless people' is a home," writes Joyce Seabolt in *Chicken Soup for the Soul, Living Catholic Faith.*

Seabolt came to that realization after volunteering for a night at a shelter. A four-in-the-morning chat with a homeless shelter guest made her realize the "elderly" guest was about her husband's age. At five a well-groomed young man hurried to wash and dress for work. He left with a brown-bag lunch to warm up the car. Meanwhile, a young woman was also dressed and left for work. Another woman thanked Seabolt for being there "and watching out for us."

At the breakfast table, Seabolt understood that "there were none of 'those people' at the table. It was just a table with 'us' around it."

Let's pray for God's guidance and show His mercy to one another.

> **The thought of my affliction and my homelessness is wormwood and gall!...(But) the steadfast love of the Lord never ceases. (Lamentations 3:19,22)**

> *Remind us, Lord, that in helping those in need we are building up Your kingdom of justice.*

Talking Strangers

On a winter night, two women leaving a Westchester, New York, train station and heading into the nearby town found themselves walking side by side.

The younger woman spoke first, noting it really wasn't too cold. The older replied: "Yes, I told my daughter that I'd walk to meet her for dinner. I just needed to breathe in the fresh air."

She then shared her fears about her husband, now hospitalized after a massive heart attack. The younger spoke of her husband, a musician and songwriter, who she wished would finally get recognized for his work.

"I'll say a prayer for your husband and for you," the younger woman said. "And I, for your family as well," added the older.

The two parted, each blessed by this one-of-a-kind sharing with another soul.

Through his faith he still speaks.
(Hebrews 11:4)

Help me see and serve You, my Redeemer, in all I meet.

History Comes Alive

Will the real Abraham Lincoln please stand up? With so many images of the sixteenth president, can we ever understand his real essence? Ryan Cole, from the U.S. Abraham Lincoln Bicentennial Commission, thinks so.

According to Cole, there are artifacts which portray "this most interesting and, arguably, most important of American lives" as a real person. A number of them were part of the Indiana State Museum's "With Charity for All" exhibit which displayed items associated with Lincoln and connected visitors to the president.

There's a cupboard Lincoln helped his father craft; his small, black legal portfolio; one of the books he owned; his inkwell and a signed copy of the Emancipation Proclamation. "These are objects he actually wore, signed or handled," Cole says. The collection unites us "to Lincoln the living, breathing man."

Search beyond image for the real person inside everyone you meet.

God gave Solomon very great wisdom, discernment, and breadth of understanding as vast as the sand on the seashore.
(1 Kings 4:29)

Reveal to me the depths of the people around me, Spirit of Understanding.

Relax, Refresh — At Home

Relax and refresh at home? Yes! Plan a no-schedule, creative, impulsive day.

Chores and responsibilities are no-no's. Stay in bed longer than usual. When you do get up, go for a massage, a swim, or a walk.

Do something that gave you joy when you were young. Not a clue? Watch children. Don't worry if it's "appropriate."

Meditate or pray quietly. Power nap. Take recess. Listen to good time music. Read a book for the sheer pleasure of it.

And don't feel guilty about your day off. "There's a huge difference between self-care and selfishness," says psychologist Dan Baker. "If you can't be good with yourself, then you can't be your best with others."

Care for your whole self as well as you care for others.

You shall love your neighbor as yourself. (Leviticus 19:18)

Jesus, remind me that I cannot love others unless I love myself and, above all, love You, the ground of my being.

An Unlikely Reunion

In the winter of 1945, Franklin W. Hobbs III was a 21-year-old corporal in the Army signal corps stationed on Iwo Jima. One day, he stumbled upon a dead Japanese soldier with an envelope sticking out of his pocket. It contained a child's drawing and a photo of a baby. Hobbs took it as a reminder of the battle.

More than 60 years later, his wife suggested they try to return the envelope to the family of the dead soldier. A Japanese friend brought photocopies of the material to Japan and officials tracked down the family. Eventually, Hobbs met Yoko Takegawa who had moved to the U.S. years before. It was her photo and drawing that her father carried with him on Iwo Jima.

"Mr. Hobbs has such a beautiful heart," says Takegawa of Hobbs' decision to return her photo and her drawing.

Reconciliation is possible. Courage is needed.

A harvest of righteousness is sown in peace for those who make peace. (James 3:18)

Divine Healer, teach us forgiveness.

Inspire the Best

Want to bring out the best in others?

You can become an instrument of inspiration. Whether you realize it or not, your words, actions, energy and even your attitudes influence those around you. By adopting a positive approach to life, you can become the type of person who inspires and elicits the best in others. Consider the following suggestions:

- Give instruction and advice in positive terms.

- Emphasize and nurture the positive qualities others have.

- Praise generously and sincerely.

- Make eye contact when you speak to others.

- Point out others' potential whenever possible.

- Instead of saying, "You shouldn't have done that," say "Try it this way next time and let's see the result."

By following these ideas, you treat your listener as an individual worthy of your full attention.

**In every way you have been enriched in Him, in speech and knowledge of every kind.
(1 Corinthians 1:4)**

Remind me, Heavenly Father, that I can positively influence others.

The Sun that Shines Above

We may not enjoy the long cold days of winter, but compared to the people of Longyearbyen, Norway, we have nothing to complain about.

Considered the northernmost town in the world, its citizens live in total darkness from mid-November until February. Then there's twilight until March when they finally see the sun. From mid-April until mid-August they experience almost endless sun.

It's no wonder that the town has a public holiday on the day the sun reappears, followed by a week-long Sunfest with concerts, exhibitions and other celebrations—and lots of parties and singing at the local pubs.

Thank God for all His gifts, starting with the sun, the moon and the stars.

Yours is the day, Yours also the night; you established the luminaries and the sun. You have fixed all the bounds of the earth; You made summer and winter. (Psalm 74:16-17)

With what beauty have You surrounded us, Creator of all!

The Positives of Surfing the Net

Much has been said and written about the downside of "surfing the Net." Some say it can become a habit, almost addictive; others say that the growth of Internet-based communications (e-mail and social networking sites) has impaired people's ability to conduct face-to-face relationships.

However, a study by the American Life Project however indicates that Internet use among older Americans may be beneficial. Over 60 percent of adults age 65 and older who use the Internet did so to research hobbies or health issues, or to make travel plans. Older Americans also find the internet appealing for social interaction and for visiting ancestry search sites. In fact, nearly 50 percent of visitors to ancestry-search sites are 55 or older.

Enjoy all the tools you have available to you, but use prudence and encourage others to do the same.

How attractive is wisdom...understanding and counsel in the venerable. (Sirach 25:5)

At every age help us to use electronic media only to enrich our lives, Divine Lord.

The Diabetic Athlete

Olympic skier Kris Freeman held onto a strong second-place in the 30-kilometer race at the 2010 Winter Olympics in Canada's British Columbia. He was just seconds away from making history as the first American since 1976 who had a shot at earning a medal in cross-country skiing.

Freeman's dreams and chances were shattered when, just seconds from completion, he collapsed. The 29-year old athlete, who battles diabetes, suddenly lost his energy in a way that only diabetics can understand.

Although Freeman knew he would not medal, he was determined to complete the race. He downed a sports drink that rescuers rushed to him and, once able to stand, finished in 45th place. As Freeman put it, "I was not going to have a 'Did Not Finish' next to my name in the Olympics."

Determination is the difference between giving up and giving it your all. When the going gets rough, keep going!

Indeed we call blessed those who showed endurance. (James 5: 11)

Strengthen my resolve to stay faithful until the end, Jesus.

Journeys of Their Own

From 1868 until 1968 Pullman porters assisted passengers during the golden age of American train travel. More than that, Lyn Hughes, curator of the Pullman Porter Museum in Chicago, says they were "the foundation of the black middle class."

One of them, Samuel Coleman, devoured copies of *The Wall Street Journal* that passengers left behind and spoke to many business leaders. Now in his 80s, he even started an investment club and aided fellow porters by spearheading unionization.

At age 18, James Smith took a job with the railroad as a dishwasher. His 12-year career on the rails was interrupted by World War II and Army service. His GI Bill education enabled him to become a civil engineer. But he insists that his "million-dollar education was on the train."

If our work is about offering our best to others, we will no doubt find much good for ourselves as well.

Keep the charge of the Lord your God, walking in His ways...so that you may prosper in all that you do. (1 Kings 2:3)

Bless all I do this day, Creator. May it give You praise.

Take the Tulip Train

Holland or New York?

During one March that might have been the question for riders of the subway train that shuttles between New York City's Grand Central Station and Times Square.

As part of a campaign to promote tourism to the Netherlands, the outside of the train car was transformed into a tulip field, with images of the area's signature bloom and windmills. Inside were more Dutch scenes, along with facts and information about its culture, people, and history. Riders were invited to enjoy the bright scenes and think about a place far from their everyday world.

Each day, we should savor the moment, right where we are. But we should also open our minds and hearts to the beauty and fresh possibilities the world over.

For a brief moment favor has been shown by the Lord our God...that He may brighten our eyes. (Ezra 9:8)

Holy Lord, in the moments of this day, may I be always in Your presence.

Bringing Hope to Refugees

It had been a busy evening on the air when radio host Delilah Luke read an unsettling e-mail. The writer, claiming to be a woman named Winifred at a refugee camp in Ghana, was asking for money to care for three children. Luke asked for more information.

The sender was actually the woman's cousin writing because Winifred is illiterate. He had heard that Luke might help. Luke reached out to World Vision, a Christian relief organization. Staffers found and aided the woman and children. They also encouraged Luke to travel to Ghana.

Distraught at the desperately crowded and disease-ridden conditions of the refugee camp, she formed Point Hope, a ministry that brings the refugees water and other assistance.

Change begins with sympathy for one person's suffering. Is there a special cause that moves you? Do all you can to help.

Have unity of spirit, sympathy, love for one another, a tender heart, and a humble mind. (1 Peter 3:8)

Awaken in us sympathy for our suffering fellow creatures, Holy Spirit.

Reviving America's Malls

In St. Louis, Missouri, the Crestwood Court mall had once been a busy commercial space. But as the recession worsened, half the stores emptied. Solution: have local artists rent available spaces to showcase their work as well as to benefit the community.

Thus ArtSpace was born. Mary Callahan, for example, is a high school art teacher who had originally planned to display her own work. Now she shares her space with her students, who frame and price their work by themselves. "All That Dance" is another site which provides rehearsal and performance space for five dance companies, including flamenco, Indian and tap dance groups.

Art gives life and culture to a community. Support the creative people who may be struggling in your own community.

He has filled them with skill to do every... work done by an artisan...designer...embroiderer... or...weaver. (Exodus 35:35)

Holy Wisdom, inspire all those whom You have blessed with artistic creativity.

Bouncing Back from Problems

Are you resilient? You are if you rebound quickly from crisis or trauma. Dr. Steven Southwick, professor of psychiatry at Yale University School of Medicine, says, "Resilient people are like trees bending in the wind. They bounce back."

The more you agree with these statements from *AARP* magazine, the more resilient you are:

- I'm usually upbeat.
- I can tolerate high levels of uncertainty.
- I adapt quickly to new developments.
- I find the humor in tough times and can laugh at myself.
- I learn valuable lessons from my experiences and others'.
- I'm good at solving problems.
- I'm strong and durable.
- I convert misfortune into opportunity and find benefits in bad experiences.

Develop your strength and resiliency.

Happy are those whose strength is in You... they go from strength to strength. (Psalm 84:5,7)

Holy Spirit, bless me with Your wisdom and courage and show me how to encourage others.

The Olympian Businesswoman

Aelin Peterson skied regularly while growing up in an Alaskan coastal village. She even made her way into the top ranks in college competition. But after she graduated, she shelved her Olympic skiing dreams and had a successful career in finance.

A visit home—and a defeat in a local ski event—pushed Peterson to want to go for the gold again. She quit her job and started training. She ended up on the U.S. cross-country ski team at the 2002 Salt Lake City Olympics. Although she did not win any medals, the experience was satisfying to Peterson.

She returned briefly to a finance career, but eventually chose to stick with what she loves. Today, she teaches skiing and is involved with a program that promotes healthy living for kids.

It's never too late to follow a dream, and always the right time to follow your heart.

Keep your heart with all vigilance, for from it flow the springs of life. (Proverbs 4:23)

Guide me, Master, that all I do may give You glory.

Finding Your Oasis

There are many ways to stay healthy. Yet one of the most important is when you press your life's "stop" button.

"If you take time for yourself regularly, you'll build calming skills that will not only improve your physical health but also boost the overall quality of your days," says Alice D. Domar, author of *Self-Nurse*.

A daily mini-getaway can reduce stress and remind you of what matters most. It may mean sitting in silence, pushing away the to-do list and anxious thoughts. Or maybe it'll be found in reviewing photographs of family and friends, reading a book, or listening to or playing music.

During these "time-outs," remember the place where we can always find refreshment – in God's loving heart.

The Lord God...will gather the lambs in His arms, and carry them in His bosom, and gently lead the mother sheep. (Isaiah 40:10,11)

Help me to slow down, Loving Shepherd.

Memories of Sweets Past

Desperately seeking the candy of your youth? Those of us who were born prior to 1965 — beware. Some of the most popular, delectable candies of the past may well be gone forever.

As candy-company monoliths took over candy making ad distribution, once-popular sweets such as Wacky Wafers, Summit Bars, PB Max, and Choco-Lites all disappeared. Regional producers couldn't keep up with larger candy companies' finances or advertising, so many smaller concerns folded. Along with them went favorites such as an old Minnesota favorite called the Seven Up and Missouri's Cherry Mash.

But there is hope for nostalgic candylovers. Web sites like Candydirect.com help candy aficionados connect with some hard-to-find goodies.

What do you miss most from your childhood? One thing's certain, most of us have a past that bears little resemblance to our present. Appreciate both, even as you plan for the future.

We will all be changed, in a moment, in the twinkling of an eye. (1 Corinthians 15:51)

Help me cope with change courageously, Jesus, my Savior.

After Tragedy, Living in Hope

Antonia Silva Lima and her family migrated to the small rain-forest village of Esperanca (Portuguese for *hope*) with other peasant farmers to embark on an experimental program to preserve the Brazilian rain forest in 2004. With the leadership of Notre Dame de Namur Sister Dorothy Stang, an environmental activist, they lived in the jungle without destroying its infrastructure or natural ecosystem.

Lima and the other farmers drew strength and encouragement from Sister Dorothy Stang who was murdered in 2005. It was she who gave the small town its name because she had been so hopeful that the pioneering project would encourage widespread eco-friendly use of the rainforest.

Lima says that "we still hope to realize Dorothy's dream of supporting our families by living in harmony with nature."

Aim to live in harmony with yourself, others, and nature.

So far as it depends on you, live peaceably with all. (Romans 12:18)

Holy Spirit, teach us peace-filled living.

That Soft, Still Voice

Almost always God speaks to us not with blazing lightning and rolling thunder, but with a small, still voice.

The story of Brother Joseph Dutton is a good example. Born in 1843, Joseph Dutton had a rough start in life: a stint in the Union Army during the Civil War, a failed marriage and a bout with alcoholism. Eventually, he turned to the Bible. He was baptized a Catholic and became a Trappist brother, but still, peace eluded him. Then, he read a magazine article about a leper colony in Hawaii that would change his life.

He traveled to Molokai to assist Father Damien De Veuster in 1886. When Father Damien died three years later, Brother Joseph took charge of caring for the lepers until his death in 1931.

A few printed words changed one man's life. How will God touch your life today?

After the fire (there was) a sound of sheer silence. (1 Kings 19:12)

Father, help me cultivate interior quietness, so that I may hear the "sheer silence" of Your voice.

Comfort to the Grieving

Losing a loved one is difficult enough, but imagine suffering such a profound loss and lacking the resources for a funeral service or even a burial.

The burial assistance program of Catholic Social Services (CSS) in North Carolina's Mecklenburg County works to address this very problem. The organization provides funeral and burial or cremation services to families in need, regardless of their faith.

Considering the rising cost of these services, the need is great. In 2009, the cost of the average burial in Mecklenburg County went from $600 to over $1,000. In response, the numbers of those in need of assistance also rose, by 40 percent. Harriet Bright, whose husband lost his battle with cancer, says, "Everybody who works at CSS is God-sent."

Comfort can come in many forms. Reach out to someone who is grieving in thoughtful and practical ways.

He will wipe every tear from their eyes. Death will be no more; mourning and crying and pain will be no more. (Revelation 21:4)

Soothe the souls that grieve, Holy Redeemer.

"Right Now" Time

During a convention, several business people chatted about the sometimes overwhelming "busy-ness" of life. Every moment seems to be packed with activity and anxiety about what has to be done next.

One woman in the group offered her solution. After years of walking that time treadmill, she had stepped off. She still maintained a full schedule, but focused on the activity at hand, not future tasks. If she was working on a project, it was that project's time. Family time was equally important and she focused on spending time with loved ones—not just putting things off until tomorrow. For her, life had become a series of "right now" times, she said.

There's a glimpse of the sacred in every moment of every day. We need to make an effort to live it—and not miss out.

Be careful then how you live...making the most of the time. (Ephesians: 5:15)

Focus my heart and mind on You, Lord.

Feeling Appreciated

Teresa Scalici loves going to work. Although she has been cooking at home for decades, it's at Enoteca Maria restaurant where patrons let her know how much they enjoy her food.

"My family has this everyday so they don't appreciate it anymore. I prefer it here because the people love me," said Scalici. "On Saturday nights the customers clap."

The Staten Island restaurant placed ads in the Italian press and hired Italian moms and grandmas to cook once a week or so. The women are experienced home cooks used to feeding big families.

"It's kind of like having dinner at your grandmother's," says one regular customer. "These are not fancy chefs, these are Italian women who know how to cook Italian food."

Doing what you love, feeling appreciated and sharing with others—the perfect recipe.

Let the favor of the Lord our God be upon us, and prosper for us the work of our hands. (Psalm 90:17)

Eternal God, urge us to show gratitude to the people around us who make our lives more pleasant day after day.

Believing in Art

The German-Czech immigrants who settled in the rolling hills of central Texas in the 19th century wanted their new-world churches to be as beautiful as old-world cathedrals.

So they tapped the talent of local artists who filled the Gothic-style churches with twining vines, surreal flowers, chubby cherubs and twinkling stars on heavenly blue ceilings.

The "Painted Churches Tour" in Schulenburg, Texas, offers a look at four such churches, with no two alike. But Texas is not the only place to see such a blend of faith and art by local artists. Hundreds of these "painted churches" can be found throughout the United States, from Vermont to California.

Everything around us inspires praise for the Creator.

From the...beauty of created things comes a corresponding perception of their Creator. (Wisdom of Solomon 13:5)

For all Your gifts to us, Father, we offer thanks and praise.

Surviving a Bad Day

Maggie was having a bad day. For starters, her alarm didn't go off, and she missed her usual bus. Outside, strong winds and driving rain put an immediate end to her umbrella.

At the train station, a broken escalator forced Maggie to trudge up 50 steps. Seated on the train, trying to shake off the annoyances, she was assaulted by sounds—music blaring through headphones of passengers and shouting from two men decrying, first, the government—and then grocery store prices!

In that moment, she got her "prayer for the day" email on her Blackberry. It read, "God, we come before you this day in the hope of experiencing your mercy and love." Amen, Maggie thought to herself, allowing herself to feel hope in her gloom.

At the core of our everyday experiences, there's always God's love. We just need to remember that.

Hope does not disappoint us, because God's love has been poured into our hearts. (Romans 5:5)

Lift my darkness, Lord; shine through with the light of Your love.

Prisoners in America

Some disturbing statistics have come to light about crime and incarceration in America.

Most compelling is the swelling prison population. The number of those imprisoned in the U.S.A. has grown to roughly 1.6 million. This means that one in every 99 adults in this country is behind bars.

Some argue that the current incarceration rate is simply too high. Non-violent offenders are often mixed in with violent criminals, thereby "recycling" petty offenders into those capable of committing worse crimes. Others say that such reports ignore the very tangible benefit of a tough-on-crime stance: lower crime rates. Indeed, the rate of violent crimes in America has fallen by 25 percent in the period from 1987 to 2007.

This is a tough problem that, like all difficult issues, deserves serious consideration and civil, constructive dialog.

You had compassion on those who were in prison. (Hebrews 10:34)

Jesus, who was crucified as a prisoner, may we imitate Your wisdom and compassion and balance justice and mercy.

Being Twenty Something

Who are the "Millennials"? They belong to a generational group defined as those born after 1980, aged 18 to 29.

A story in *USA Today* notes they are "less church-connected than prior generations were when they were in their 20's. But just about as spiritual as their parents and grandparents were at those ages." While Millennials are "significantly more likely than young adults in earlier generations to say they don't identify with any religious group," many pray often, believe God exists, and say religion is important in their lives.

They vote at a higher rate; they're more ethnically and racially diverse. Just 21 percent are married; that's half the percentage of their parents' generation at the same age. Yet many consider marriage and family high priorities.

Each generation brings a fresh perspective. Encourage people of all ages to be the best individuals they can be.

O God, from my youth You have taught me, and I still proclaim Your wondrous deeds. (Psalm 71:17)

Help me to appreciate the gifts of all your children, Eternal Father.

Molding Opportunity

In 1849, John Caldwell Bloomfield inherited an estate, which encompassed the entire village of Belleek in the west of Ireland.

The Potato Famine had broken the people there, in body and spirit, and Bloomfield sought a way to help them. One day, he noticed that the exterior of his tenant farmers' cottages had a vivid white finish. Bloomfield was told it was from the unusual clay found on his land that was used in the construction of the homes.

Within a few years, Bloomfield built a factory to make pottery from that clay, incorporating Irish designs and producing a translucent glass-like finish. An immediate success, Belleek ware is today a multi-million dollar industry.

Even in the worst of times, there's a solution shining through somewhere, just waiting for us to shape it to success.

Who will separate us from the love of Christ? Will hardship, or distress, or persecution, or famine, or nakedness, or peril, or sword? ...No, in all these things we are more than conquerors through him who loved us. (Romans 8:35, 37)

Lord, You formed me and know me; remain with me.

Let's Enjoy Time and Life

Parents. Overscheduled? Of course. Over-worked? Ditto.

And your children? They probably are, too. Besides school, extra-curricular activities and even play-dates are scheduled. Yet spontaneous play time often teaches children to explore the world, experiment with rules, work together with others and solve problems. It improves their ability to learn, teaches social and emotional skills and gives them exercise.

So, how can you make your life and your children's lives less hectic? Allow no more than two scheduled activities per child and parent. Guard family time like the treasure it is. Make family nights a regular part of everyone's life. Let your children see you strolling, daydreaming, or lost in a book.

You and your children have one life. Live it gently.

Observe the sabbath day and keep it holy...so that (all) may rest. (Deuteronomy 5:12,14)

Remind us, Lord, that life is for living, loving and being, not just doing and producing.

Beyond Sheer Genius

Albert Einstein, Nobel laureate and physicist, known for his theory of relativity, is frequently cited as an example of genius. But he was more than a great scientist. He had a real insight into human nature, as witnessed by some of his quotes:

"Setting an example is not the main means of influencing another, it is the only means."

"To punish me for my contempt for authority, fate made me an authority myself."

"I never think of the future. It comes soon enough."

"The individual who has experienced solitude will not easily become a victim of mass suggestion."

"It is the supreme art of the teacher to awaken joy in creative expression and knowledge."

Einstein understood that we are each individuals with something to contribute to the world. What are you contributing?

The good person out of the good treasure of the heart produces good. (Luke 6:45)

Father, help me use Your gifts with generosity and wisdom.

A Purim Celebration

Welcome to the party—on the bus.

The Purim Party Bus is a mobile festival, the creation of rabbis of the Chabad-Lubavitch movement. It's their way of helping students at five colleges in Massachusetts observe this Jewish holiday with fanciful costumes, joyful music and feasting. Guests at the bus party receive a small gift of food, a Purim custom.

Purim recalls Queen Esther's courageous actions which saved her fellow Jews from a plot to destroy them by Haman, an advisor to the king of Persia.

"It's wonderful that Purim is coming to us," said one student.

Life is filled with reasons to celebrate. Spread the word!

Keep the fourteenth day of...Adar and also the fifteenth...days of feasting and gladness...sending gifts of food to one another and presents to the poor. (Esther 9:21,22)

Thank You for liberating us, God.

Making a Difference in Simple Ways

Ever notice how the most potent changes frequently come from those who reach out to others in simple ways?

While Susan Farmer was battling an advanced stage of breast cancer, she derived healing and hope from the beautiful garden that was planted in her own yard by a group called Hope in Bloom, founded by Roberta Dehman Hershon.

Hershon believes in the healing power of flowers. That's why she founded the Massachusetts-based non-profit organization that has planted more than 70 gardens (including the one enjoyed by Farmer who remains in remission) to help cancer survivors heal. "My goal is to bring smiles, joy and a sense of renewing life," says Hershon. "I want to send a message: There is hope."

Simple kindness and generosity make the most difference in others' lives. Build these acts of service into your daily life.

Like good stewards...serve one another with whatever gift each of you has received. (1 Peter 4:10)

Inspire us to serve others with Your gifts, Blessed Trinity. Help us to share kindness and beauty with Your people.

When Disaster Hit Her Home

A disaster preparedness expert for a consulting firm, Joan Bishop of Fairfax, Virginia, seemed ready for anything—earthquakes, hurricanes, epidemics, and the like.

Then the H1N1 virus—the swine flu—landed on her own doorstep, infecting first her 10-year-old, Beri, and then her older daughter, Bailey, 13.

As her girls grew sicker, Bishop was overwhelmed with anxiety at what would happen next. Her expertise intensified her concerns. "I know too much," she thought.

Both children eventually recovered, although her older daughter still has some continuing health issues. And Bishop now has a lasting impression of the human emotions behind a given disaster or pandemic.

No matter the knowledge we acquire, our actions are always affected by our feelings and personal relationships.

I saw the Lord always before me...therefore my heart was glad, and my tongue rejoiced; moreover my flesh will live in hope. (Acts 2:25-26)

Gather us in, merciful Redeemer. Rescue us!

A Recipe for Life

Jacques Pépin seems to have lived a charmed life.

In his autobiography, *The Apprentice: My Life in the Kitchen*, this master chef writes of his rise from a cook in his mother's restaurant in rural France to the author of 21 cookbooks and the star of 13 cooking shows on television. He tells of cooking meals for prime ministers and four-star generals, and of spending time learning from the best chefs.

But Pépin's book is about more than preparing food. His tender memories and thoughts, said one critic, will bring you to tears, and make you laugh out loud. "We all wish we could cook like Pépin," the reviewer noted, "but this enchanting tale will make you wish you knew him."

In our own lives as well, it is more important how we accomplish things than what we actually do. With love in the mix, life is always worth savoring.

By this everyone will know that you are my disciples, if you have love for one another. (John 13:35)

You fill me with good things, Paraclete; You are to be praised.

Dressing the Tresses of Opera's Stars

Like most major entertainment events, an operatic performance requires the effort and know-how of sometimes hundreds of professionals and workers—most of whom remain behind the scenes.

Take Nina Lawson. For more than 30 years, Lawson ran the wig department at the Metropolitan Opera in New York. She tended to the elaborate hair pieces of great opera stars such as Maria Callas, Renata Tebaldi and Roberta Peters.

On occasion, Lawson had to contend with temperamental egos. Yet she was known for her grace, professionalism, and perfection: Not one of the wigs she fitted ever toppled during a performance.

Give credit to the unsung workers in your life. A kind word can go a long way.

Take courage all you people of the land, says the Lord; work, for I am with you, says the Lord of Hosts. (Haggai 2:4)

May I recognize and express my appreciation for the labor of others, Jesus of Nazareth.

On a Knee to Know Basis

Sue had had trouble with her knees for several years. Physical therapy and other treatments had proved fruitless. Her doctor scheduled knee replacement surgery for just three weeks away.

Frightened and questioning, Sue looked for answers among knee replacement support groups on Facebook. She found Marie.

They connected online, by email, and eventually by phone. Before surgery and during recovery, Marie was there for Sue, answering questions, offering advice, and, most times, just listening to Sue's fears and frustrations.

"You've been like a guardian angel," Sue wrote in one message to her newfound friend. "So glad to have found you."

In a world of endless possibilities for connecting with others, it's important to make connections count—one person at a time.

Faithful friends are life-saving medicine. (Sirach 6:16)

Merciful Savior, hear my prayer. Bless me with friends and angels.

A Different Kindergarten

Cold rain. Leaden sky. Bundle yourself and your young children up and head out doors? Or turn on the heat and the TV?

The youngsters who attend the Waldorf School of Saratoga Springs spend three hours a day outdoors with their teachers regardless of the weather.

Waldorf teacher Sigrid D'Aleo says that their large motor skills develop, they work out their social issues in a better way and their play is more imaginative. Richard Louv, author of *Last Child in the Woods*, says children get to use all their senses simultaneously without overtaxing them.

Kim Lytle loves the idea of her 3-year-old being outside daily. She adds that with the proper gear it's healthy "to experience the elements and brave the world—and not just on a sunny day."

Allow God to gift your children with His Creation daily.

The streets of the city shall be full of boys and girls playing. (Zechariah 8:5)

Encourage parents to introduce their children to Creation in all seasons and weathers, Creator.

Re-creating Life

Lissa Lowe worked crazy hours and traveled the world in her advertising career. Then her mom became sick.

Lowe took a leave of absence, remaining by her mother's side until her final breath—a moment, she says, that helped refocus her own life.

Lowe stepped out of the fast-paced, stress-filled ad world, and tapped her design and art skills. She sketched sweet, simple images for children's clothes—and Fuss Frocks was born.

Another moment—the birth of son Charlie—pushed her to rethink life's direction again. Spruce Decor is Lowe's effort to help others combine high end and thrift store items to decorate at home.

Take time to review your own life's direction. You just may pinpoint a possibility for a better tomorrow.

I know that there is nothing better for (workers) than to be happy and enjoy themselves as long as they live. (Ecclesiastes 3:12)

Abide with me, Abba, guiding my every day decisions.

A Beggar for the Poor

Lucious Newsom so loved serving the poor and helping others that, in his seventies, he went from Tennessee to Indianapolis to volunteer at a soup kitchen. That was the beginning of a nearly two-decade career of service.

Newsom offered poor people dignity in addition to his tireless energy and complete faith in God's goodness. His neighbors loved him in return as they watched the retired Baptist-minister bringing food and companionship to the neediest in the community and generally making lives better. When Newsom died at age 93, he was still putting in 14-hour days.

The pastor of one Indianapolis church said, "He was very serious when he introduced himself as a beggar for the poor. He was truly able to see the face of God in the needy."

A life of service is rich in fulfillment and meaning.

Sing the praises of...godly men, whose righteous deeds have not been forgotten. (Sirach 44:1,10)

Lord, remind us that material wealth is fleeting; spiritual riches, everlasting.

Enriching Lives by Welcoming Others

Maura and Carnie Nulton's fifth child, Charley, was born with Down syndrome. His parents feared he would not be able to attend school with his siblings, because their parochial school lacked special-education resources.

The Nultons decided to brainstorm with the parents of other special-needs children in their Kansas City neighborhood. Today, the Kansas City-St. Joseph diocese in Missouri has the Foundation for Inclusive Religious Education (FIRE), which provides grants to seven parochial schools and one high school with special-needs students.

"All the students have benefited" says a school official. "It has created a richer environment and it has been an education in itself."

Root out your subtle prejudices. By welcoming those who are unlike us into our lives, we live more fully.

Whoever welcomes one such child in My Name welcomes Me...and the One who sent Me. (Mark 9:37)

Bless those who live with an open heart, Father.

I Can See Clearly Now

For two days one March, travelers through New York City's Grand Central Station couldn't help but see things more clearly. During that time, the station played host to a display of eyewear in its Vanderbilt Hall.

The exhibit included the oldest documented pair of eyeglasses—invented in 13th century Italy—as well as possibilities for improving vision in the future. Eyeglasses worn by celebrities were also available for viewing.

The display, sponsored by Italian eyewear manufacturers, highlighted the quality, craftsmanship and innovative design of that country's glasses throughout history.

All around us are inventions that make our lives easier, as well as solutions to the challenges of any day. Remember to take a good look around.

Lift up your eyes to the heavens, and look at the earth beneath; for the heavens will vanish like smoke, the earth will wear out like a garment...but My salvation will be forever. (Isaiah 51: 6)

Blessed Trinity, show me Your kindness and mercy. Help me help others to see the same.

The Experience of Homeless People

Unfortunately, the problem of homelessness continues, so it's heartening to know that a new generation is eager to learn about the people it affects most.

Students from the Catholic campus ministry program at the University of Texas in Brownsville participated in a social justice project on homelessness, which included time living outside and asking strangers for money.

"A lot of people laughed at us and others walked by like they didn't care," said one student.

"Some people were rude but most just walked by and said 'No thank you.' We felt rejected," said another.

On the other hand, other passers-by showed compassion, asked questions and made donations.

Knowledge and empathy alone won't end homelessness. How well do you understand the experience of living without a home to call your own?

To teach...knowledge and prudence to the young — Let the wise also hear and gain in learning. (Proverbs 1:4-5)

Spirit of Knowledge, teach me to think and learn about the problems of Your suffering children.

Being Positive About Pranks

Psychologists have studied pranks for years, most often in a negative context, related to harassment, bullying and the like.

But pranks and practical jokes can help bring individuals into a group; temper success with humility; or by stirring self-reflection, function as a check on arrogance or obliviousness.

"Being duped…" explains Kathleen Vohs, a psychologist at the University of Minnesota, "may in fact show people where they are on the scale— too trusting or too vigilant."

Neal Roese, a University of Illinois psychologist, explains that self-examination after a prank can "kick start" new behaviors and self-improvement.

We should never deliberately hurt or humiliate another person. And we should always make sure our actions reflect God's love for ourselves and for our neighbors.

Love…God with all your heart…soul and…mind… Love your neighbor as yourself. (Matthew 22:37,39)

Holy Spirit, guide my choices and actions.

For a Living Memory

Jewish prisoners incarcerated in Philadelphia's notorious Eastern State Penitentiary from 1924 until 1970, could practice their faith, regardless of the crimes they had committed.

When the prison closed in 1970, severe water damage spoiled the tiny synagogue, which then remained abandoned for years. The rich woodwork rotted; the plaster, including a large Star of David affixed to the ceiling, crumbled.

Today, known as the Alfred W. Fleisher Memorial Synagogue, the little synagogue and its kitchen (where outside Kosher food was served on holidays) have been restored, and are open to the public.

Measuring just 31 feet by 17 feet, the once-forgotten space holds a wealth of tradition, memories and historic significance.

Whoever they are and wherever they are, respect others' faith traditions.

Pay...respect to whom respect is due....Owe no one anything except to love one another. (Romans 13:7,8)

Instill in us respect for others' beliefs, Adonai.

Divine Assignments

After 20 years of conducting cancer research, Dr. Linda Malkas still remembers something she heard in church decades ago. The senior minister of her church said, "When God sees a problem, He puts people on earth to fix it."

Malkas took that statement to heart, particularly when her beloved father died of cancer. Her grief turned to steady resolve, and she embarked on a career as a cancer researcher. "Maybe it was my way of grieving, but I found myself wanting to learn about the disease that took my father's life," she says.

Today, she has made great strides in identifying proteins that play a key role in DNA replication, a critical aspect of cancer research. "I knew cancer research was what I was meant to do," she says.

What job does God have in store for you?

To each is given a manifestation of the Spirit for the common good. (1 Corinthians 12:7)

Lord, bless those who serve You by serving Your people.

Putting an End to Garbage

Across the United States, there's a new trend—"zero waste"—as various venues resolve to remove all signs of refuse.

At Yellowstone National Park, for example, clear soda cups and white utensils are made of plant-based plastics which dissolve when heated for a few minutes. And the Honda Motor Company is recycling so diligently that many of its factories have gotten rid of their trash dumpsters.

The movement to recycle and compost is strong at many corporations, restaurants, stadiums, national parks, and school cafeterias. Reaching into the average household with the message is the next step.

God created the earth and its abundance, and asked us to care for it. Don't throw away your chance to be a good steward of creation this very day!

Be exalted, O God, above the heavens. Let Your glory be over all the earth. (Psalm 57:5)

I give praise to You, Creator of all that I see.

Home Saver

Marilyn Mock attended a foreclosure auction, prepared only to encourage her son, a first-time home buyer. She ended up buying a house and giving it back to its original owner.

Tracy Orr, a single mom, happened to sit next to Mock at the auction and shared her story. Now, Orr repays Mock a little bit each month.

Mock and her husband, Bruce, own a small construction company. In fact, she refinanced their dump truck to pay for Orr's home. The mortgage crisis and its accompanying sad stories moved her to launch the Foreclosure Angel Foundation to help other homeowners facing the loss of their homes.

"Marilyn didn't just give me back my house," Orr says. "She gave me back my faith that one person can make a difference."

Our actions can help someone find joy or relieve worry and sorrow.

Stretch out your hand to the poor. (Sirach 7:32)

In suffering, Eternal Father, I trust in Your mercy and love.

With Eyes Turned Upward

Jesuit Father George V. Coyne understandably has his sights aimed toward Heaven. Yet there's another reason he looks upward. The retired director of the Vatican Observatory has studied the wonders of outer space for more than 50 years.

He earned his doctorate in 1962 for his study of the chemical composition of the moon's surface, and thereafter established his role as a leader in the field of astronomy.

When asked what propelled him toward a lifelong study of the skies, he said, "I had a teacher of Latin and Greek who often became distracted, and talked about astronomy." It was during those interludes that Father Coyne discovered his passion for planets.

What sparks a hunger for learning in you? Follow your heart and pursue what you love with enthusiasm.

The heavens are telling the glory of God; and the firmament proclaims his handiwork. Day to day pours forth speech, and night to night declares knowledge. (Psalm 19:1-2)

Turn me in the direction of the path You have set before me, Yahweh.

Students Against Sweatshops

Russell Athletic is a leading sportswear company. After its employees at a Honduran factory unionized, the company closed the factory, forcing 1,200 workers out of their jobs.

This sparked students to begin a nationwide campaign against the company. Their coalition, United Students Against Sweatshops, persuaded the administrations of 96 colleges and universities, including Harvard, Stanford, and New York University, to suspend or sever their licensing agreements with the company. As a result, Russell agreed to rehire the 1,200 workers who had lost their jobs.

Moises Alvarado, a union leader in Honduras, states, "We are impressed by the social conscience of the students in the United States."

Fight for the rights of those in greatest need.

When human rights are perverted in the presence of the Most High, when one's case is subverted — does the Lord not see it? (Lamentations 3:35-36)

Remind us, Lord, that You look to us to remedy the injustice that injures our brothers and sisters wherever they live.

Warm, Snuggly and Comforting

Most cancer patients are warned that they will lose their hair from chemotherapy, but not that it could hurt. Pam Haschke, a Chicago breast-cancer survivor, says, "My scalp felt like little pins were stinging it."

As she healed, Haschke wanted to make this aspect of cancer treatment easier on others. She knitted 200 baby-soft woolen caps for local cancer patients. "The commitment to make one cap is not huge, but the impact is so great," she believes.

Now, she's started Chicagoland Head Huggers, a volunteer group that knits and crochets thousands of caps and sends them to oncology centers around the country. Most importantly, patients know they are not alone. "They realize that someone cares—someone who knows what they're going through," says Haschke.

Small acts of love can bring great joy. No deed is too small to make a difference in the lives of others.

I was naked and you gave Me clothing, I was sick and you took care of Me. (Matthew 25:36)

How can we help people with serious illnesses, Jesus?

Excuse or Opportunity?

It's been said that perception is reality. This may be especially true when it comes to poverty.

Consider Brazilian percussionist Carlinhos Brown. Brown recalls growing up in Candeal Pequeno, a community in Salvador, Brazil where he made music by banging on water barrels. He used to carry them home to his mother, who earned a living washing clothes. Back then, Brown's neighborhood had so many fruit trees that a kid would go hungry only if he could not climb.

Once he earned fame and fortune, Brown set out to help alleviate the poverty which had overtaken his hometown. He started a music school and a civic association to bring practical help and dignity to his former neighbors. But he stands firm that "Poverty is not an excuse for anything; it is an opportunity."

How do you perceive life's challenges?

Honesty comes home to those who practice it. (Sirach 27:9)

Strengthen me, Father, to work hard and achieve honorably.

Another Recession Casualty: Charities

It's no secret that during our recent recession consumer spending has gone down and charities have been hard-hit. As the world economic crisis has worsened, even those who wish to give to the needy are faced with hard choices: How much can I give? And to which cause?

One way to deal with this problem is through a "giving circle" which is an informal group of donors who pool contributions to support a common cause. The structure of the group can be highly flexible, and usually requires only that members generally agree on the purpose and target of donations.

Creativity can go a long way in tough times. Try to set aside as much as you reasonably can to assist those in need, whenever possible.

Do good...be rich in good works, generous, and ready to share,...take hold of the life that really is life. (1 Timothy 6:18-19)

Broaden the reach of our works, Divine Master, so that we may help those in need.

Haute Couturier from the Bronx

Think of renowned clothing designer Ralph Lauren and images of haute couture, the finest fabrics and hefty price tags likely come to mind. Few know that Lauren (born Ralph Lifshitz) was raised in the Bronx. His parents were Russian-Jewish immigrants who worked hard to provide for their family.

When reflecting on the relatively modest means that marked his childhood and what inspired his interest in design, Lauren, a public school student, says that he noticed the clean, crisp uniforms of local prep-school students. "I was always impressed by their classic look. Maybe because I didn't have it, I reached for it."

Rather than envy what others had, Lauren used their achievements as an impetus for his own ambitions.

Turn any envy you feel into inspiration to succeed.

Work...diligently. (Ezra 5:8)

Remind me that I should not covet what others have, God.

From Mountains to Board Rooms

They began as perhaps the two men least likely to head up million-dollar corporations: Doug Tompkins and Yvon Chouinard were mountain-climbing fanatics back in the 1960s. Their passion for heights dominated their lives, taking them on extensive climbing trips around the world.

When the two traveled to South America they documented their travels with photographs and film. Soon after, each started a corporation based on their experiences. Tompkins founded and eventually sold his North Face company, then, with his wife, built the Esprit clothing enterprise. Chouinard eventually formed Patagonia, another outdoor-clothing concern that promoted environmentally conscious business practices. Both of them are deeply involved in conservation issues.

Treasure your life's experiences. Each and every one of them may be the beginning of a new venture.

The mountain of the Lord's house shall be established as the highest of the mountains. (Micah 4:1)

Help me see opportunities in life experiences, Holy Redeemer.

Keeping Life Interesting

Sometimes it rains—an endless deluge of life's trials and disappointments.

On this particular day, Ann felt defeated by those challenges. Then she scrolled through the messages on her BlackBerry, coming across an e-mail from a missionary friend in Africa.

"It's raining now a bit," he wrote, describing the weather. "The direct road is closed, so we take the longer route through town and the market. It's always interesting."

It's true, Ann thought. Sometimes the direct road in life is blocked, and a clear path to peace of mind seems nowhere in sight. But, as her friend observed, the longer route, although more challenging, offers us a chance for "interesting" possibilities, encounters with those around us that may help lighten our load.

The best defense against life's "rain" is an open heart, open enough to recognize and welcome such encounters when storms blow us off course.

Then they cried to the Lord in their trouble, and He brought them out from their distress. (Psalm 109:28)

Lord, send Your light, to shine through our darkest days.

Making Sound Media Choices

You can use the media to enrich your children's imagination, foster their social and moral development and help build a secure sense of self. Try some of these ideas:

- Read, listen to or view media that interest your children.

- Ask your children what techniques are used to attract their attention; what lifestyles and viewpoints are included or omitted. Set age appropriate time limits and rules for television, internet, video games, etc.

- Offer magazines and books that empower children to think critically, develop knowledge and widen their views.

- Explain the logic behind your positions.

Most importantly, give good example, not mixed messages.

The Lord honors a father above his children, and He confirms a mother's right over her children. (Sirach 3:2)

Help parents and children be discriminating consumers of the media, God.

Crows and Us

Lyanda Lynn Haupt, the author of the book *Crow Planet,* writes "an intimate awareness of the continuity between our lives and the rest of life is the only thing that will truly conserve the earth—this wonderful earth that we rightly love."

She asks how we are connected to the earth and how we are to live on this changing earth. And she reminds us that we cannot know the results of our actions unless we know all our neighbors, human and animal. After all, we live on a planet beyond our cultivated places and our minds' and yards' edges.

Begin to know, to understand, and to live well alongside the wildlife with whom we share this earth. You are part of the natural ecosystem.

Every wild animal of the forest is Mine, the cattle on a thousand hills. I know all the birds... and all that moves in the field is Mine. (Psalm 50:10-11)

Creator, remind us that we are part of Nature, not above it.

Sad Memories Spur Compassion

Despite a natural urge to forget such tragedies, many of us remember the horrific 2007 shootings on the Virginia Technical Institute campus in which 33 people, including the gunman, died.

Bryan and Renee Cloyd have gone a step further. Their daughter, Austin, was one of the victims of the tragedy. Yet, they have managed to find a way to channel grief into positive action for the benefit of others.

The Cloyds asked that donations in Austin's memory be sent to a program that repairs dilapidated houses in the poorest parts of Appalachia. To their surprise, the program received nearly $70,000 almost immediately after they announced their request.

"We realized there was no better therapy than doing more to help others," they said.

The grief that comes with the loss of loved ones may never disappear. But this family demonstrates one way to help cope with such deep sadness.

Thus says the Lord...as a mother comforts her child, so I will comfort you. (Isaiah 66:12,13)

Cradle the grieving in Your arms of comfort, Abba.

Sabbath Peace!

Observant Jews take the Sabbath seriously. No phones, no newspapers, no work, no carrying anything. It is a time to be; to love and be loved, to rest; to worship, to enjoy life.

Jesus said the Sabbath was made for people. What does that mean? All work and no rest can lead to depression at never-ending chores. On the other hand, if rest ends in boredom, that's not healthy or helpful to our bodies and souls either.

So observing the Sabbath acknowledges that God is God. And that our individual worth comes from being His children, not merely from what we do. Celebrating the Sabbath also means worshiping the Lord with our neighbors.

Keep a weekly Sabbath. You and God are worth it.

Remember the Sabbath day and keep it holy. (Exodus 20:8)

God, help me and my loved ones to observe a holy Sabbath.

Burger King and Child Champion

"The two most important days of your life," says Tom Walsh, "are the day you were born and the day you figure out why you were born."

In the case of this South Dakota native, the latter was the day he committed himself to working with children with debilitating diseases.

The businessman who operates Burger King and TCBY restaurants in the Dakotas and Minnesota, had traveled to Los Cabos, Mexico for years. While Los Cabos had a highly developed tourism industry, Walsh realized that its health-care system, especially for children, was poor.

He established the Los Cabos Children's Foundation to provide world-class medical care to local children. Now his efforts are improving lives, one child at a time.

What's your purpose? This could be the day you find out!

Worship the Lord your God, and serve Him only. (Matthew 4:10)

How may I serve You this day, Lord? Guide me.

Fighting Back — No Matter What

On April 19, 1943, German troops were preparing to send the last 60,000 Jews in the Warsaw ghetto to their deaths. However, on that particular Passover Eve, the Germans met a surprise: the start of the Warsaw Ghetto Uprising.

Marek Edelman was one of its leaders. He had watched the Nazis deporting Jews at the rate of 6,000 a day. He knew that despite the promise of resettlement, they were murdered.

He helped form the Jewish Combat Organization, which fought back on that fateful Passover Eve. "We knew we wouldn't win; we fought simply not to allow the Germans alone to pick the time and place of our deaths," said Edelman.

He remained a resistance fighter until the end of the war. Afterwards, he became a doctor and, in the 1980's, was active in Poland's Solidarity movement. He died at age 90 in 2009.

Sometimes the effort, not the outcome, matters most.

Fight the good fight. (1 Timothy 6:12)

Remind us, Father, to fight the good fight for ourselves, our families, our nation and our faiths.

Doing the Necessary

Paige Byrne Shortal believes that God doesn't put a task in front of us without the means to accomplish it. But, cautions the Missouri native, we have to cooperate with God. Here are a few of her rules to do just that.

1. **Make choices.** Time's limited; activities are endless. Set goals about what you want to accomplish.

2. **The people in front of you are most important.** Life "online," virtual living, can dominate your day. Instead, we should focus on the real live people around us.

3. **Do today's work today.** God gives us what we need to accomplish today's task. If we don't have what we need, is it yesterday's job or tomorrow's work that we're worrying about needlessly?

For every duty, we're fortified with our share of God's own boundless love.

> **By wisdom a house is built, and by understanding it is established. By knowledge the rooms are filled with all precious and pleasant riches. (Proverbs 24:3-4)**

> *For You, Lord, all things are possible; give me a share of Your strength.*

Suffering's True Make-Up

Paralyzed and near death.

That was the experience several years ago for Father Jan Michael Joncas, a Catholic priest and composer of liturgical music, including the well-known song "On Eagle's Wings." He spent months in the hospital regaining the use of his arms and legs.

The incident, he said, gave him insight into suffering, and through that suffering, into his connectedness to God and others. He went from "pondering God" to "experiencing God."

His musical compositions now center on rescue, hope and thanksgiving. And, he admits, he's much less concerned about his agenda and about getting feedback from people. He is, in fact, better able to just enter into the world of his neighbors and be with them, even if it just means being present and silent.

When we suffer, our cry for help is always heard, by a loving God who sends us His strength.

Heal me, O Lord, and I shall be healed; save me, and I shall be saved; for you are my praise. (Jeremiah 17:14)

Renew my spirit with Your love, Divine Master.

In the Sign of the Cross

Nobel Prize-winning author Alexander Solzhenitsyn was imprisoned for a number of years in Soviet labor camps. One day, at the point of despair, he dropped his shovel, sat down on a bench and closed his eyes. He did not care anymore if a guard killed him.

Hearing footsteps, he looked up to see an elderly prisoner who knelt down and with a stick scratched the Sign of the Cross into the dirt. In that moment Solzhenitsyn realized that he was not alone. The power of the cross gave him the hope to go on.

The Sign of the Cross is not only a reminder of the Holy Trinity and of the redeeming death of Jesus, but of God's all encompassing love for each of us who are indeed His children.

Use this sign of faith, hope and love to remind yourself of our Lord's divine mercy.

Through (Jesus) God was pleased to reconcile to Himself all things...making peace through the blood of His cross. (1 Colossians 1:20)

Grant Your mercy to me, Holy Trinity, and to all Your people, especially those most in need of Your strength.

Blessed Are Those Who Wait

For weeks, Debra Tomaselli, a writer who lives in Altamonte Springs, Florida, worked hard to deepen her relationship with God. No matter how much she prayed, attended church or volunteered, "He felt distant and untouchable."

This all changed when Tomaselli underwent minor surgery. While she was bedridden, she read a book called *Divine Embrace* by Ken Gire. Gire had also experienced a spiritual dry spell, and later wrote, "God had indeed been silent. But silent in the way an artist at work is silent. He had been quietly at work in me, forming Christ in me."

These words helped Tomaselli realize that God works in mysterious ways. By being patient and taking the time to meditate, we can strengthen our relationship with God and our loved ones.

Even when He seems far away, put your trust in the Lord.

Trust in the Lord forever, for in the Lord God you have an everlasting rock. (Isaiah 26:4)

Lord, grant me wisdom so I can learn to fully appreciate you.

Pray — and Draw Closer to God

Prayer is a lifting of your mind and heart to God. It might be at set times, or spontaneous. It might be in moments of solitude or when surrounded by others. But this union with God is prayer nonetheless.

Develop your love language with God: trace the Sign of the Cross on yourself or loved ones. Heed Jesus who said: "When you are praying, do not heap up empty phrases." (Matthew 6:7) A few sincere words can be enough.

Read the Psalms, and as phrases strike you, try to commit them to memory. For example, "Be exalted, O God, above the heavens." (Psalm 57:5)

Remember that while your requests might not always be answered, your prayers always will be.

Never cease thanking, praising and speaking with God.

Let my prayer be counted as incense before You. (Psalm 141:2)

Holy Wisdom, teach us to pray and to rejoice in Your presence always and everywhere.

Giving Body and Soul

Msgr. Eric Powell is one clergyman who has literally dedicated body and soul to his ministry.

One Easter Monday, Msgr. Powell donated one of his kidneys to a parishioner during a two-hour surgery. He was up and walking around the same day, eager to connect with the recipient.

While there's always a chance of failure with a kidney transplant, the pastor was encouraged when his doctor told him that he had "a nice looking kidney." Powell knew it was a rare opportunity, and seized it on learning of his parishioner's need.

"In 19 years of priesthood, I was never made aware of a parishioner with a similar need," he says. "I just didn't want to see someone suffer when I had something that could potentially alleviate that suffering for one, possibly two decades."

Your time and talents, your kindness and concern are yours to share. Be generous.

The measure you give will be the measure you get, and still more. (Mark 4:24)

Show us how to be genuinely generous, Spirit of God.

Hotel Heroes

Three Massachusetts college students returned to their Acapulco, Mexico, hotel room after an evening out, ready for some rest. Suddenly they heard the sound of glass shattering, and black smoke seemed to be everywhere. A fire had broken out in one of the hotel's laundry chutes.

Almost all of the hotel's 502 rooms were filled with American college students on spring break. "I thought of their parents," recalls Daniel Moreno. "It motivated me."

Immediately, he and his companions, Brian Stanley and Drew Nalewanski, went from floor-to-floor, banging on doors, and directing people out of the hotel. In the end, no one was seriously hurt.

Not every action needs to be heroic. But our thoughts, words and deeds—when other-directed—always make a difference for the better.

How precious is your steadfast love, O God! All people may take refuge in the shadow of Your wings. (Psalm 36:7)

Master, keep us safe when away from home.

Running for Life

Michelle Nikitaides did not let a diagnosis of follicular lymphoma beat her. With the constant love and support of family and friends, Nikitaides endured chemotherapy and came out cancer-free. She even had a favorite phrase to keep herself going: "Be a positive thinker, not a negative stinker."

Nikitaides has been in remission and has raised $12,000 for blood cancer research. She also runs in marathons sponsored by the Leukemia and Lymphoma Society (LLS). Her initial role in LLS's Team for Training was to inspire and mentor marathon runners as an "Honored Hero."

Then she realized she wanted to run to show that she really was a survivor. Nikitaides trained for and completed the marathon with a friend using the inner strength she found through her cancer challenge to carry her through each mile.

Use the pain and problems of your own life to grow.

Hope does not disappoint us. (Romans 5:5)

Help us be hopeful, Wisdom of Ages.

Model Ambassador

Katie Ford once ran Ford Models, one of the world's most famous modeling agencies. Her life changed when she joined a women's leadership group that was studying human trafficking. Since then, she has given up her career to be an unpaid ambassador in the fight against modern day slavery.

The cause suits her well. "The target age is 14 to 24, so it's similar to modeling," she states. "I knew how to reach that market." Ford also uses her connections in the fashion business to spread awareness. For example, she had eight models record messages about human trafficking for Ford Models' annual Supermodel of the World contest.

What sacrifices can you make to benefit people in need? How can you use your gifts for a cause in which you believe ?

Love...God with all your heart...soul...mind, and... strength....Love your neighbor as yourself. (Mark 12:30,31)

Adoni, may whole-souled love be at the heart of all I do.

Quietly Changing Young Lives

Father Flanagan's Boys Town is well known as a place where troubled young people improve their lives with adult guidance and peer support.

Less well known is the story of Henry Monsky, a prominent Jewish lawyer who provided crucial financial support in the Town's early days. He preferred his role to remain quiet, according to Van Varner in *Guideposts.*

Started in Nebraska in 1917, Boys Town epitomized Father Flanagan's vision of a home where youngsters would learn important life skills while helping themselves and others.

"Evidently Monsky believed that the highest form of charity came through helping someone in need anonymously," writes Varner. "This distinguished man, once the international president of B'nai B'rith and a key figure in organizing the American Jewish Conference, established one of his greatest legacies through his silent support of Father Flanagan."

How can you quietly aid someone today?

When you give alms, do not let your left hand know what your right hand is doing. (Matthew 6:3)

Remind me to be generous without needing the gratitude of others, gracious Lord.

An Extra Special Prom

Coping with serious illness is a burden. Add the unique challenges of adolescence and you get an idea of what Ashley Riemer is confronting.

She has leukemia and is getting through her ordeal with the support of family, friends and staff at Walter Reed Army Medical Center. But she was unable to attend her senior year in high school or attend her prom. So they brought the prom to her. According to *USA Today*, "plans snowballed from what was originally going to be a little dance with a jukebox and snacks to a full-out formal party with a live DJ and catered food."

Dozens attended. A professional applied her makeup creating the illusion of lashes lost to chemotherapy. Individuals and charities donated everything from limos to gowns. Ashley's whole family was overwhelmed by the outpouring of generosity.

Surely there are people in your community who could use your kindness and creativity.

You will be enriched in every way for your great generosity. (2 Corinthians 9:11)

Jesus, help me to imitate Your overwhelming mercy to my brothers and sisters in pain or in trouble.

Change Your Life In Five Steps

Bob and Melinda Blanchard know a great deal about reinventing themselves. After all, they've done so several times over the course of their changing careers, having founded and pursued a number of businesses.

The Blanchards, authors of *Changing Your Life: the 5-Step Guide to Getting the Life You Want*, recommend some ideas to anyone considering a career change. First, decide what you want to do. Make up your mind that you want to create change.

Then research and explore all the "what ifs" of your new venture. Act: put your dream into action; don't just think about it. Finally, remain flexible and open to adjustments. New careers, business ventures and life-altering plans take time to become established.

There are no guarantees in life, but you will certainly never achieve a goal unless you give it all you've got.

Get wisdom. (Proverbs 4:5)

Inspire us to remain open to new ideas, Holy God.

Unjust Expectations

According to Kathleen Deveny writing in *Newsweek* magazine, women and girls often suffer "the soft bigotry of high expectations." What does that mean?

- Women are not expected to be as violent, rude or crude as men may sometimes be.
- Boys-will-be-boys, but girls and women are expected to be neat, clean and courteous.
- On the job, women are supposed to be better behaved and more honest, but less tough and decisive than men. They are also cheaper: earning only 80 cents for every dollar paid to a man.

Perhaps one day each girl and boy, woman and man will be seen as a unique individual. Do what you can to bring that day closer for all of us.

With the judgment you make you will be judged. (Mathew 7:2)

God of all, guide women and girls, men and boys in respecting one another.

No Fortune Cookies Here

Three billion fortune cookies are made each year. They are served in Chinese restaurants the world over—but not in China.

The reason? These cookies probably originated in Japan. At least that's the theory of researcher Yasuko Nakamachi.

She's turned up references in Japanese literature and history to these prophetic treats, including an 1878 etching of a man making them in a bakery. That's decades before reports of the first American fortune cookies, which seem to have made their way here during World War II. Japanese immigrants started serving them up in their restaurants along with Americanized Chinese cuisine.

No matter its origin, the fortune cookie has been a fun final note to many a meal, proving that good ideas are meant to be shared and savored by all.

Extend hospitality to strangers. (Romans 12:13)

Nourish me with Your wisdom; let me live in Your love, Lord.

Blind, Not So Handicapped

It's amazing that Michael Hingson and his guide dog, Roselle, safely escaped the collapsing Twin Towers on Sept. 11, 2001, in New York City.

But surviving those attacks was just one more stereotype-busting feat for Hingson who is blind. "I grew up in a family where my parents insisted that I had the same responsibilities as everybody else," he says. "I understood that my life was what I was going to make of it. So I worked."

He earned a Masters degree in physics, got married, and became a regional manager at his firm. Hingson now devotes himself to the Guide Dogs Association where he encourages independence for blind children.

"Blindness isn't the problem," he says. "It's the prejudices and short-sightedness of sighted people that cause the problem."

Let's not let our biases injure people who, like us, are just doing the best they can.

Why do you see the speck in your neighbor's eye, but do not notice the log in your own eye? (Matthew 7:3)

Remind me to treat others with the respect I want for myself, Blessed Trinity.

Business for the Greater Good

If you think that the aim of all college business majors and MBA students is to develop careers where they can make as much money as possible without worrying about anybody or anything, think again.

Some students at Harvard Business School introduced "The MBA Oath" at graduation in 2009. The voluntary pledge says that the goal of business is to "serve the greater good" and that they will act with integrity and not put "their own narrow ambitions" ahead of other people.

Students at Columbia University have similar plans. The University of Pennsylvania's Zicklin Center for Business Ethics is sponsoring student clubs to discuss this vital topic.

Whatever our job, each of us has a responsibility to act ethically and for the good of all our brothers and sisters.

Commit your work to the Lord. (Proverbs 16:3)

Help me choose to live morally and compassionately at work, at home, wherever I am, Gracious Father.

What's a Mother To Do

Alarm bells sounded every time Claire thought of her daughter Elizabeth's friends. One pre-teen in particular seemed troubled.

With loving encouragement from her mom, little by little, Elizabeth spoke about her own worries for that friend. Claire knew what she had to do; she called the other mom.

"I want to share some things about your daughter with you—out of loving concern," she began the conversation. The two talked—and sometimes cried—for more than an hour, as the other mom spoke of her struggles, feelings and fears.

"Can we keep talking in the future?" she asked Claire as the initial conversation ended. "Absolutely," she replied.

It's sometimes hard to wade into the problems of others. But life's burdens become lighter when carried together—with love.

Blessed be the Lord who daily bears us up. (Psalm 68:19)

When I am weary, Loving Lord, send me rest.

"King" of This High-School Prom

Brother Kenneth Hoagland was desperately concerned about what he saw at the annual senior prom for students at Kellenberg Memorial High School in Uniondale, New York. Excessive spending as well as after-prom alcohol and sex seemed to dominate the event for most students.

Hoagland proposed to school leaders and parents that the school withdraw its sponsorship of the prom. Hoagland received 5,000 letters, only 19 of which opposed his idea.

Today, Kellenberg High's senior prom is a dinner-dance cruise around Manhattan. Only Kellenberg students may attend, and alcohol, limos, tuxedos and formal gowns are prohibited. The whole evening costs each student roughly $130, not the $1,000 some students used to spend.

Teach teens by example that a good time doesn't depend on excess.

Better is a little with the fear of the Lord. (Proverbs 15:16)

Remind adults to set teens an example of temperate yet joyful living, Abba.

Combining Clouds and Angel Hair

Let's talk about moms.

That's what some second graders did, answering questions from "why did God make mothers?" to "what are mothers made of?"

In answer to the latter question, one child said, "angel hair, clouds and everything nice in the world." On the other hand, another youngster added, "and one dab of mean." One second grader thought God made mothers for a really practical reason: "She's the only one who knows where the scotch tape is."

And when asked what it would take to make their mothers perfect, one little one replied, "On the inside she's already perfect."

Mom or dad, uncle or aunt, brother or sister or friend, we're all called to lovingly nurture the people around us.

Whoever does the will of God is my brother and sister and mother. (Mark 3:35)

Help me to find You, Lord, in the hearts of those who surround me—and help them find You within me.

Why Wait?

Most of us feel pretty good about celebrating Mother's Day, Father's Day, and other official days of appreciation. Who wouldn't feel good about acknowledging people we love?

But an online organization called HelpOthers.org promotes appreciating others— even strangers—and expressing love and gratitude every day. Here are some of the unique and fun suggestions in their Index of Kindness:

- Beautify public places. Help clean up litter; erase graffiti.

- Give a homemade sandwich to a homeless person.

- Send thank-you notes to local community volunteers.

- Surprise a family member with a random act of kindness.

- Call a longtime friend to say "I love you."

Remember, love, kindness and appreciation do not stop and start with the days on a calendar. Express them hour-by-hour.

If I...do not have love, I am a noisy gong...I am nothing...I gain nothing. (1 Corinthians 13:1,2,3)

Infuse us with loving kindness and compassion for each other, Prince of Peace.

Persistence Pays Off

After attending college for 20 years, Anita Sokol was more than ready to receive her bachelor's degree. The 62-year-old mother and grandmother took evening and weekend classes at New York City's Queens College while raising a family and working full-time.

Sokol acknowledged the support of family and friends in helping her achieve her educational goals. She noted that her former boss, who attended the commencement ceremonies, had allowed her to rearrange her work to accommodate her class schedule.

Sokol singled out her late mother for special praise. "She taught me to never stop learning."

It's amazing what we can accomplish if we keep our goal in mind and have persistence.

Give instruction to the wise, and they will be wiser still; teach the righteous and they will gain in learning. (Proverbs 9:9)

Never let me give up on myself or my efforts to learn about Your world and its people, Creator of all.

Wild, Wonderful Plants

Plants cover our earth and have amazing abilities that extend far beyond their ability to add green to our surroundings.

Some coat themselves in a glossy wax, while others can grow a furry covering resembling hair. Still others can sprout spiky spines that serve as a unique, armor-like form of protection. They come in all shapes, textures and sizes, and many display qualities that serve to invite—or repel—human touch.

Take the "Red Head" fountain grass, or the chenille plant, as examples. Both are considered soft and fuzzy plants, gentle to the touch. Yet their fluffiness enables these plants to better disperse seeds and grow plentifully. Then there's the flocked, silver foliage of alpine plants like lamb's ears; the outer layer locks in moisture and safeguards them from too much sun.

What a wondrous world we live in! Respect and preserve nature's beauty and bounty.

The Lord...gives showers of rain to you, the vegetation in the field to everyone. (Zechariah 10:1)

Thank you, Father God, for the beauty of Earth.

Reminders of Home

It's natural for people to try to re-create cherished reminders of home, no matter where they are. Rincon Criollo in the Bronx is a small clubhouse nestled in a community garden where residents gather to cook, make music, and otherwise re-create the casitas or "little houses" common in the Puerto Rican countryside.

"This is an important place for the community because it helps it to remember its roots," said one man sitting inside the wooden building.

There's an effort underway to declare Rincon Criollo a city landmark, according to *The New York Times*. Urban planner Bernd Zimmermann told the Times that casitas were established because "Puerto Ricans wanted to recreate their villages to stabilize themselves while adjusting" to life in New York City.

Create a nurturing home life and neighborhood and share a lifetime of fond memories.

**The Lord will make you a house.
(2 Samuel 7:11)**

Help me to remember the past even as I build for the future today, Creator of all.

Taming the Wild

Jennifer Steager always wanted to own a horse. When the opportunity arose, she adopted a wild mustang and began the slow process of building a relationship of trust.

Indigo was one of a group of wild mustangs brought to Saint Mary-of-the-Woods College in Indiana which has a notable equine program through the U.S. Bureau of Land Management. When the horses arrived, they wanted to jump out of the pen and bite. Only consistent care could calm them.

At first Indigo wouldn't let Steager near him. But every day for weeks, she patiently cleaned the stall, fed and trained him. They built a trusting relationship.

"I see a lot of God's patience and love in me trying to work with the horses, and also in what they return to me," says Steager.

Trust takes time and patience, but in all relationships, it's worth it in the end.

Those who trust in the Lord are like Mount Zion, which cannot be moved, but abides forever. (Psalm 125:1)

Show me how to trust You and Your word, merciful God.

Making Sense of Sensational Stories

If you get panicky when you read newspapers or hear news reports, you've got company. Many stories seem designed to make us fear for our lives and our world—and maybe they are.

According to Simon Briscoe and Hugh Aldersey-Williams, authors of *Panicology: Two Statisticians Explain What's Worth Worrying About (and What's Not) in the 21st Century,* we should worry less. Why? Information presented as facts may have come from biased studies or may only reveal a tiny part of the truth.

They suggest that we ask ourselves if people making statements have a vested interest in the issue. And we should question why a story is appearing right now; for example, stories on global warming often appear in the middle of summer.

What's in print, on air or on the Web, isn't necessarily true. Exercise good judgment daily.

How attractive is sound judgment. (Sirach 25:4)

Bless us with Your wisdom, knowledge and understanding, Paraclete.

The Reluctant Missionary

Donna Ryckaert listened as her friend Jean related stories about her medical mission work in Guatemala. Suddenly, Jean suggested Ryckaert try such service.

"Who me? Mission work?" Ryckaert recalls thinking.

Pushing reservations aside, she went to Guatemala for a week, traveling with a group that included three doctors and her teenage son. They found poverty and great need, but also generous hearts, and unparalleled faith and love of God. Since then she has returned several times and encouraged others to go.

But what does such missionary service really mean to the people? It's a sign of hope, a missionary nun assured her—a message that people outside their world cared enough to take time to be with them.

Opportunities abound to help our neighbor; sometimes we just need to take that leap of faith.

The apostles said to the Lord, "Increase our faith!" (Luke 17:5)

I want to be Your messenger, Father, to give witness to Your love.

Spiritual Daycare

When Guardian Angel Daycare opened in Draper, Utah, a number of years ago, the purpose was to create a safe and nurturing environment for children. Many parents were local teachers who wanted a place where youngsters' Christian values could grow.

Guardian Angel Daycare has helped children prepare for the future by offering basic math, reading and religion courses. They even have reunions for old classmates. Some former classmates are so grateful that they come back to serve as volunteers when they are older.

All children deserve an environment that protects them while encouraging their social, educational and spiritual development. Help the children in your life become decent human beings who will spread the word of God.

All may go well with you and your children after you, because you do what is right in the sight of the Lord. (Deuteronomy 12:25)

Lord, grant me the power to help teach my children to be loving individuals.

De-clutter Your Life

The National Association of Professional Organizers found in a recent study that 65 percent of people agree that their households are "moderately disorganized." Still, there are good reasons why you should take the time to put your home in order.

First, organization will help you save money. Rearranging the items in kitchen and closets allows you to see what you already have, preventing you from making needless purchases.

Second, purging your home of clutter increases your efficiency. Keeping unwanted files on your computer and piles of paper on your desk can be distracting and prevent you from finding information that you really need.

Finally, organizing the space around you helps revitalize your energy and concentrate on what you really want to do.

Use that new energy to live positively and productively.

Be careful then how you live. (Ephesians 5:15)

Holy God, help us remove the clutter from our homes, offices and lives to better serve You — and to enjoy life more.

A Convent Goes Green

When the Episcopal sisters of the Community of the Holy Spirit decided to build a new convent in Manhattan, they planned it with one specific color in mind—green.

The convent will have rooftop gardens, water heated by solar power, rainwater collection, natural light and ventilation, and the use of environmentally sensitive materials throughout.

"It's a question of stewardship," says Sister Faith Margaret, explaining the motivation for their choices. "Of responsibility."

While their new convent is being built, the sisters continue their green ways, recycling, composting, eating organic produce and using energy-efficient light bulbs.

We, too, are called to protect and preserve God's creation. Today and every day, conserve, clean up, and cherish the exquisite mystery and beauty that surrounds you.

It is required of stewards that they be found trustworthy. (1 Corinthians 4:2)

When recycling, composting, and other green actions seem tedious, Spirit of Life, refresh our sense of stewardship.

Standing on Faith

Gina Gilday is a catcher for the Elms College softball team in Massachusetts. In fact, Gilday has played softball for more than a dozen years. That's nothing unusual—until you discover that Gilday was born without legs.

"My parents are amazing," she explains. "They brought me up to have strong faith and believe that God would never give you anything you can't handle."

Gilday is also a volunteer tutor and works in customer relations for a bus company. She drives a car with hand controls and wants to be a high school teacher.

"I work with what I have and go with that," she says.

Each of us has strengths—and a share of shortcomings too. The key is to build on what we have and count on God for the rest.

**Wisdom gives strength to the wise.
(Ecclesiastes 7:19)**

You formed me and You know me, Lord. Be my strength.

Stress Busters

A messy house, an unreliable friend, and noisy kids—would you accept these "little things" as a part of your daily life?

Most people probably would, but these annoyances contribute to stress that's harmful to your body. Stress hormones are useful when they help people in life-threatening situations. But if you are always stressed out, your body constantly releases these hormones, which can result in diabetes, heart disease, cancer, and depression.

Eliminate the small stressors that plague your life. Take simple steps. For instance, schedule a 10-minute "pickup time" for the family to get rid of daily clutter. Take a relaxing shower. Be kind but assertive with rude salespeople. Avoid arguing with your spouse. Remember that everyone is entitled to his or her own opinion—and personality quirks.

Don't dismiss potentially harmful stressors. Take care of yourself so that you can take care of others.

There is no wealth better than health of body, and no gladness above joy of heart. (Sirach 30:16)

Remind us to have a healthy care for our selves, God who commanded us to love our neighbors as we love ourselves.

The Sheep and the Weeds

On a Montana mountainside a flock of sheep graze on 1,000 acres of public land. But these sheep aren't just eating—they're feasting on the weeds infesting the area.

Nationwide, sheep grazing is gaining popularity as a low-cost, nontoxic tool in the battle to control a variety of weed species. Plus their dung is free fertilizer.

"It's environmentally friendly," says Jeff Mosley, an extension range management specialist at Montana State University. "Grazing has an aesthetic appeal and a bucolic aspect. It's a natural form, and people appreciate that as well."

These wooly herbivores can be found nibbling away in places like the Civil War battlefields of Virginia, the ski slopes in Vermont, and the vineyards in California.

As with sheep, each of us has gifts that can benefit others. Discover and use yours wisely.

We have gifts that differ according to the grace given to us. (Romans 12:6)

Thanks for the gifts You've given to us and to Earth's creatures, Good Shepherd.

Lifelong E-Learning

"I couldn't believe all of this was available—for free," says Stan Peirce.

The retired electrical engineer unexpectedly discovered a wealth of information on the Massachusetts Institute of Technology website. MIT and other notable institutions put much valuable material online with free access to the public. You can find everything from academic lectures including assignments and syllabuses to language lessons and basic how-to videos.

"I think we're entering an era where lifelong learners will have access to limitless amounts of free, noncommercial educational opportunities. Arguably, we're already there," said Dan Coleman, who directs Stanford University's continuing studies program.

If you don't have a computer, visit your local library. Most have equipment available to the public.

Keep using your God-given gifts and never stop learning.

May my teaching drop like the rain, my speech condense like the dew; like gentle rain on grass, like showers on new growth.
(Deuteronomy 32:2)

Teach me, Paraclete, Your ways and Your wisdom.

The Ultimate Goal

In 1964, 36-year-old Canadian Jean Vanier, a former naval officer, sought a way to follow Jesus and live the Gospel message.

So he bought a house in Trosly, France, named it "L'Arche," and invited two intellectually disabled men to live with him. Today, more than 132 L'Arche communities exist in 34 countries. They welcome people of all faiths and are designed to treat the intellectually disabled with respect.

Vanier believed that "each person is important. Even if you cannot speak, even if you cannot walk, even if you've been abandoned, you have a gift to give."

The ultimate purpose of life is not merely to focus on the self and to foster internal growth. On the contrary, each person needs to share his or her gifts with others and to appreciate their talents and uniqueness.

There are varieties of gifts. (1 Corinthians 12:4)

Holy Spirit, help us appreciate each other.

From Dust to Digital

Lance Ledbetter had always been a gospel music enthusiast. He never guessed that he would one day receive Grammy nominations for preserving historical American Gospel recordings.

In 2003, after several years of extensive research, Ledbetter released *Goodbye, Babylon*. This six-disc box set contains 134 early twentieth century Gospel songs. Along with a 200-page book of liner notes, the set is packed in raw cotton in a cedar box.

The next year, this album received Grammy nominations for Best Historical Album and Best Boxed Package. Following this success, Ledbetter made his label, Dust-to-Digital, a full-time venture, under which he resurrects the music of American blues, jazz, and folk artists.

It's important to preserve the artistic heritage of a culture.

**Wine and music gladden the heart.
(Sirach 40:20)**

May we hear echoes of your loveliness in music, Ancient of Days.

Dig In!

Stephen Orr, who writes for *The New York Times,* makes the case for gardening without using gloves: "I like to feel what I'm doing. I want to grasp the wiry, waxy bundles of knotweeds as I tug them out of the ground. I have to feel that the daffodil bulb that I'm burying is firm, juicy, and safe in its papery tunic."

It's important to dig our hands into soft earth for the purely physical sensation. "My preference for hands-on gardening is not without its downside," Orr writes. "My fingers ache with the cold when I plant my hundred plus bulb order."

And yet, "In a world where digital information zips untouched around the globe and paper books may not be held in our hands for much longer, I can replace my usual cerebral work with the gritty, muddy, slightly painful joys of the purely tactile."

Use all your senses. Touch the world you live in.

They shall be like a tree planted by water, sending out its roots by the stream.
(Jeremiah 17:8)

May I use my hands to celebrate Your glorious universe, Eternal God.

The Power of Art

The cathedral of Notre Dame de Chartres is one of the best examples of Gothic art and architecture in the world.

Malcolm Miller's love for the French cathedral influenced his whole life. His attachment began in 1956, while studying for a degree in French at England's Durham University. After graduating, he took several teaching jobs in France, but returned to Chartres as a guide every Easter and summer break.

Then he became ill. Finally, in 1968, after six operations and seven months in a hospital, Miller traveled back to Chartres. Upon seeing the cathedral, he wept. Now a prominent interpreter at the cathedral, Miller continues to show its treasures to visitors. He has also written several guidebooks on Chartres and its cathedral.

Whether a building, a painting, or any work of art—make time to appreciate beauty.

Behold the beauty of the Lord. (Psalm 27:4)

For all that's beautiful thank You, Beauty ever ancient, ever new.

God, All Around Us

Do you wish to experience God's presence?

Jesuit Father William Barry, writing in *America* magazine, reminds us that "At every moment you are in the presence of God. So you must seek to take a contemplative stance toward the world. Pay attention to what you encounter in your ordinary life, and you will experience God's presence."

In other words, just be attentive to everything around you. That means something as familiar as that gnarled tree in the backyard. Really see, feel, smell and touch its rough ridged bark. Or, consider a friend's body language and looks and not just the words when he or she speaks about something important.

Gerard Manley Hopkins wrote, "The world is charged with the grandeur of God." Pay attention and appreciate the world and its Creator.

Listen to Me...My hand laid the foundation of the earth, and My right hand spread out the heavens; when I summon them, they stand at attention. (Isaiah 48:12,13)

Help me be attentive to You within myself, others, and all Creation, loving Father.

From College to Community

The ink was barely dry on Gretchen Sneegas' diploma from Indiana University when she enlisted in AmeriCorps National Civilian Community Corps, an organization that dispatches volunteers to disaster areas within the United States.

Sneegas is among a growing population of recent college graduates who, instead of going straight into paid positions or to graduate school, are opting for community service and volunteer work. "In today's economic recession, the need for community service is greater than ever," she says.

She adds, "Being a good Catholic means more than simply going to Mass once a week," alluding to the critical importance of serving others as part of her faith.

Don't let the sun go down on an opportunity to serve others. Make it a part of your daily life.

The greatest among you must become like the youngest, and the leader like one who serves. (Luke 22:26)

Help me grow in kindness and compassion, Prince of Peace.

A Voice of Conviction

Musician Pete Seeger turned 90 years old in 2009, and many say that his youthful appearance belies his age.

While he indeed has a devoted bank of fans worldwide, he has also had his share of critics. That's because Seeger was not only a musician throughout his career, but also a political activist who ruffled the feathers of many powerful politicians and policymakers.

In the 1950s, Seeger was blacklisted and refused to cooperate with the House Un-American Activities Committee and was nearly jailed for contempt. By the late 1960s, his career had revived, and he continued to sing songs of protest and to champion the importance of civil rights and protecting the environment.

While we may not support the opinions of others, find agreement in our mutual right to express our opinions.

Do not speak evil against one another, brothers and sisters. ...There is one Lawgiver and Judge who is able to save and to destroy. So who, then, are you to judge your neighbors? (James 4:11-12)

Increase our tolerance for one another, Savior.

Finally, Recognition They Deserve

Connecticut's 29th Regiment wore the blue cotton uniform other Union soldiers wore. But the free black farmers, bricklayers and delivery men of the 29th were denied rifles and bayonets; paid less than half their promised wages; and camped in open fields without tents. Like white soldiers, bloody battles, injuries, disease and death were their lot.

Sharpened sticks were their weapons; their officers were white. Yet, on April 3, 1865 the Connecticut 29th was the first Union regiment to enter Richmond, Virginia, the capitol of the Confederacy.

Harrison Mero, a retired affirmative-action program director and great-great-grandson of a soldier of the regiment, led a campaign for a fitting memorial to the men of Connecticut's 29th regiment. It was finally unveiled in New Haven in 2008.

Have zero-tolerance toward all forms of prejudice.

God said, "Let us make humankind in our image, according to Our likeness." (Genesis 1:26)

Jesus, remind us that we are all children of the one Father.

Building Hope

Over 20 years ago, Christine Brady was recovering from a bad marriage. To help herself get through the difficult time, she decided to take on a challenge. So she went to Mexico, working at an orphanage where 40 percent of children leave school before fifth grade.

"I realized how much help the kids needed," Brady says. She quit her engineering job and determined to build a school for kindergarteners in Tijuana. The success of the kindergarten has led to the construction of an elementary school and a high school. These schools offer a full curriculum of dance, music, art, ecology, computers, English, French, nutrition and exercise.

Brady's own daughters are so proud of her that the youngest says, "My sisters and I will make sure that what she has accomplished will live on."

Nourish children's bodies and minds as often as you can.

Who, if your child asks for a fish, will give a snake...for an egg, will give a scorpion? (Luke 11:11,12)

How can we help children, especially poor, neglected and abused ones, Lamb of God?

A Flower's Power

According to Greek mythology, Aphrodite named the rose. The floors of Cleopatra's palace were said to be carpeted with its delicate petals. And the wise Confucius had a 600-book library specifically on its care.

The rose is also the official floral emblem of the United States where June is national rose month. While the flower bears no fruit, rose hips, the part left on the plant after a rose has finished blooming, contain more vitamin C than almost any other fruit or vegetable.

This beautiful bloom can be found on the oldest living rose bush—1,000 years old at best guess—still flourishing on the wall of the Hildesheim Cathedral in Germany.

The beauty of God's creation is meant to bring us joy, calling us always to preserve and protect it.

Now the winter is past, the rain is over and gone. The flowers appear on the earth; the time of singing has come, the voice of the turtledove is heard in our land. (Song of Solomon 2:11-12)

Lord, I give You thanks; You have given me all good things.

Learning Peace

Peace building, explains Patrick Corrigan, is not about programs but about helping people become connected.

The Ohioan got an intense chance to do just that shortly after his graduation from the University of Notre Dame. As part of an internship with a group promoting peace in Uganda, he sat in on a meeting between government officials and rebel leaders.

Negotiations broke down, but the experience and the relationships made pointed Corrigan to a purpose in life—helping victims of conflict—and strengthened his faith.

"These people still believe in God; they still have joy," he said. Their faith "deepened my experience of Jesus and what it means to follow him."

We meet a spark of the Divine in each person. Remain open to experiencing those glimpses of God's light and love.

**God created humankind in His image.
(Genesis 1:27)**

Creator, help us recognize You in others.

A Most Unusual Wedding Registry

When Leora Madden and Tony Gambell announced their engagement, loved ones were surprised by the couple's choice of wedding registry gifts.

Rather than stock their wedding-wish list with china, crystal and silverware, the couple invited friends and family to purchase building materials for a Habitat for Humanity home in Bay St. Louis, Mississippi, Madden's hometown. They plan to help build it and then give the house to a needy family.

The couple says that the homebuilding organization itself is one reason the two got together, and ultimately, married. "We both felt we already had everything we needed," says Madden. "This was a unique opportunity to give to others."

Generosity of spirit is a blessing not only to the person who's receiving but, perhaps even more so, to the giver. Open your hands and your heart to others.

You will be enriched in every way for your great generosity, which will produce thanksgiving to God through us. (2 Corinthians 9:11)

Increase our capacity for being openhanded and gracious, Christ, our Savior.

Healthful Eating By Example

Many people these days are paying attention to the rise in obesity in the United States and the need to encourage good nutrition among children and adults.

First Lady Michelle Obama is among them, emphasizing the importance of healthful eating for all. She praises community vegetable gardens and she has invited the press into the White House kitchen to highlight her own preferences for healthful, low-fat, low-calorie meals for her family.

"She thinks communities across the nation deserve to have access to fresh fruits and vegetables," says a food magazine editor.

Each of us needs to take responsibility for the food we choose to enjoy. Start a trend. Treat yourself and your family to healthful eating, and encourage your friends and neighbors to do likewise.

Daniel asked the guard..."Let us be given vegetables to eat and water to drink." (Daniel 1:11,12)

May respect for our bodies lead us to healthful eating and temperate living, Divine Creator.

Time Out for Recess

Remember your schooldays? Remember rushing through lunch so you could go out to play? Some schools are testing the idea of recess first, and it seems to be paying off.

North Ranch Elementary in Scottsdale, Arizona, was one of the first to try the switch on the advice of their school nurse. The school tracked changes and discovered that far less food was wasted since the children weren't trying to finish quickly to go outside. Visits to the nurse also dropped 40 percent with fewer reports of headaches and stomachaches.

Other schools are also pleased. About one-third of Montana's schools changed schedules and report more relaxed eating and improved behavior among students.

Sometimes it pays to shake things up a little and experiment with new ways of doing things. Think about your own situation. What might you change for the better?

**Listen, I will tell you a mystery! We will not all die, but we will all be changed.
(1 Corinthians 15:51)**

Father, transform me into the person You want me to be.

A Revolution for the Amish

Since coming to North America in the eighteenth century, the Amish have maintained their simple lifestyle and avoided modern technology. But with the rising cost and decreasing availability of farmland, the Amish find their values challenged as they are forced to operate small businesses for income.

Through their ventures, the Amish have upheld their traditional values of integrity, high quality, and hard work, which have earned their business a failure rate of less than 5 percent. In order to run these enterprises, many Amish use computers and cell phones, but they keep their work and home lives separate to keep a tight rein on technology.

When we find ourselves in unfavorable circumstances, we can, with the support of our family and our community, uphold our values and do our best to prosper.

Remember...the covenant that He made with Abraham. (1 Ch. 16:15,16)

Help us to uphold our values—Your Covenant—in difficult times, Lord of Sinai.

Drawing Hope

The students at St. Mary's School in Middlebury, Vermont, decided to raise awareness of genocide in the Darfur region of the Sudan. They painted a canvas tent.

Their artwork joined 400 other such tents on the National Mall in Washington, D.C. one weekend in 2008. The "Tents of Hope" were then sent to a refugee camp in Chad in Africa to be used as classrooms.

"When we as people of faith come together to work for peace and justice," explains Rev. Tim Franklin, pastor of Bridport Congregational Church in Middlebury and one of the local organizers, "we show that we take our faith seriously and that we truly love our neighbors as ourselves."

Each of us is called to make a difference every day—for neighbors near and far.

Thus says the Lord of hosts: Render true judgments, show kindness and mercy to one another. (Zechariah 7:9)

Bring justice to Your world, Master; cover the universe in Your love.

Courage, Big or Small

What does the word courage mean to you? Grand, large-scale acts of heroism? Saving a life? Small but significant acts that change lives and have a long-lasting effect?

Courage can mean Rosa Parks refusing to comply with a Montgomery, Alabama, ordinance restricting African Americans to the back of city buses.

Or, courage can be telling the difficult truth to a loved one. Or it can mean volunteering at a center for abused children. Or refusing to enable a loved one mired in addiction. Or confronting one's own addictions, and seeking help.

Courage takes many forms: public, private; big, small. Celebrate your own bravery and that of the people around you. Every act of unselfish, loving courage does make a difference.

Be courageous, be strong. Let all that you do be done in love. (1 Corinthians 16:13-14)

Give me a share of Your own courage, Jesus.

Leading by Example

Most people know of Bonnie Raitt, a Grammy-Award winning songwriter, singer and musician. Older folks and fans of Broadway musicals remember her father John Raitt's acclaimed performances in *Carousel, Oklahoma! The Pajama Game* and other hits.

Bonnie Raitt calls her dad "the most important influence" in her life, and not primarily from a musical or performance aspect. She says that her father's commitment to family, friends and celebrations such as Christmas and Thanksgiving shaped her own values.

"He lived his principles in his actions, and was the most positive person I've ever met," she says of her late father. "He never complained, never spoke badly of anyone."

Such principles are simple, yet they left an indelible mark. Live by example, and inspire change in others.

Become an example to all.
(1 Thessalonians 1:7)

Gracious God, lead me to a life that is pleasing to You.

Holding Onto Hope

The 250-tent Pinellas Hope Camp in St. Petersburg, Florida, has been at full capacity since it opened in 2007. A literal city of tents, the camp provides temporary shelter for hundreds of homeless people aged 18 to mid-70s, a need that was magnified by the economic downturn.

Despite their circumstances, however, residents at Pinellas Hope are filled with, well, hope. "This is a great place to be," says one resident. "It's safe, and beats sleeping on the street. It gives us a great opportunity."

Says another resident, "The people are really wonderful."

It takes character to remain hopeful and grateful in hard times. How do you react when life is at its most difficult?

They remained resolutely hopeful.
(3 Maccabees 2:33)

Teach me gratitude, restraint, composure and patience, Redeemer.

Dealing with Difficult People

Are you responsible for handling conflicts between people on the job or elsewhere? Professional mediators use specific methods when dealing with sensitive issues. The Iowa Mediation Service, for example, offers these techniques:

1. Affirm and validate. People need to feel heard, understood and appreciated.

2. Make the parties responsible for their words and actions. Be aware of nonverbal cues.

3. Slow down the conversation. Lower your voice. Relax your body. Take breaks.

4. Be silent. Give everyone time to think.

5. Set limits. End the discussion if parties aren't respectful.

6. Model good behaviors and be an active and involved listener. Show you're committed to problem-solving.

These are skills worth developing for all of us. Always make an effort to understand and respect those around you.

Honor everyone. (1 Peter 2:17)

Help me to be patient with others and to treat them as well as I want to be treated, my Savior.

A Student's Teacher

Fifty students in one first-grade class. That was the situation facing teachers at a Brooklyn, New York, public school in 1932. City officials said there was no money to build an addition to accommodate the growing student population.

Helen Weinstein, there in her first teaching job, launched a protest. She organized the parents, distributed leaflets—printed on the school's mimeograph machine—and took part in protest parades. In the end, the school got its addition, so that each class had fewer students for a better learning environment.

Weinstein, like many teachers who put their students first, continued to stand up for them throughout her career.

Situations around us, big and small, demand action. Don't miss your call to make a difference today!

Keep alert, stand firm in your faith, be courageous, be strong. (1 Corinthians 16:13)

Teach me Your ways, Lord, that I may serve You well.

Ready To Help

"I've never really thought twice about helping people," said Coast Guard Petty Officer First Class Lavelas Luckey. "If you think you can do something to help, then you just do it."

Luckey has even risked his own life to help others. One day on his way to work in Glen Burnie, Maryland, he rescued a five-year-old girl from a car engulfed in flames. Luckey came upon a three-car pileup that claimed the girl's mother and left the child trapped in the car seat. Luckey struggled to free her while surrounded by flames. "The danger didn't really hit me until later that night" said the rescuer.

It's not necessary to risk your life in order to help others. If you are alert for opportunities, you can be helpful in small everyday ways: give up your seat on the bus, hold open a door, smile and say a kind word.

The Lord will rescue me from every evil attack and save me for His heavenly kingdom. (2 Timothy 4:18)

Help me to save others from sorrow, pain and loneliness by reaching out to them with compassion, Spirit of Love.

History Threatened

The National Trust for Historic Preservation has a list of endangered historical sites that need attention immediately. These include:

Memorial Bridge. Considered the longest vertical lift bridge in the U.S. in 1923, it links New Hampshire to Maine.

Dorchester Academy. In 1871 a school for emancipated slaves, it remains Georgia's center for civil-rights and African-American progress.

Mount Taylor. Located in New Mexico, it is a holy place to many Native Americans.

Respect and help conserve these and other sites that represent America's history. They are yours!

Let us now sing the praises of...our ancestors. (Sirach 44:1)

Teach us to know and treasure our history and heritage, God of all nations.

Famous Feline

When Dewey's amazing story began, no one guessed how it would ultimately unfold.

In 1988, librarians in Spencer, Iowa, discovered a shivering kitten wedged in the library's book drop. They rescued and adopted the cat, naming him Dewey Readmore Books through a write-in contest. With love and nurturing, the orange tabby settled into his new home and became a hit with patrons.

"By the time he was two, he was in local papers and on TV," according to former library director Vicki Myron. "His pictures started appearing everywhere."

Dewey showed up in magazines, on radio, even film documentaries. After his death 19 years later, his obituary ran in papers around the world. That's when Myron wrote the bestselling book, *Dewey: The Small Town Library Cat Who Touched the World*.

The kindness of strangers changed Dewey's life. His life, touched others. Take a lesson from that.

Show kindness and mercy to one another. (Zechariah 7:9)

Help me show compassion to all people and to all creation, Blessed Trinity.

Pass The Comfort Food

Chicken-and-stuffing casserole, veggie pasta shells, hamburger-comfort casserole. These are just a few of the items on Peace Lutheran Church's menu.

Known as Peace Meals, the program is run by volunteers. Rev. Pat Eidness, associate minister, saw the program in action at another Sioux Falls, South Dakota, church and decided to imitate a good idea. "The beauty is that it involves the whole congregation," says Rev. Eidness. "It really has brought people together."

One pastor donated a freezer; some congregants buy groceries and provide cookware and aluminum foil. Still others cook or deliver the frozen meals to any local person in need of a good, hot meal. Recipients get the casserole along with a list of ingredients, heating instructions and a prayer.

With physical, emotional and spiritual nourishment as ingredients, this ministry has found a winning recipe—one worth sharing.

See the food with which I fed you in the wilderness, when I brought you out of the land of Egypt. (Exodus 16:32)

Show me how to extend Your mercy and generosity to those in need of loving kindness, Savior.

Men's Night

Eric Utne's 18 and 23-year-old sons were leaving home. Utne asked male friends to gather and share their insights with his sons. Here are some of them:

Learn about the plight of others. Tend relationships like gold. Work out issues sooner. Express love, kindness, feelings. Work to improve your emotional intelligence. Understand relationships with teachers, students, others. Develop practical skills and intellectual ones. Balance self-confidence and humility, curiosity and independence. Trust yourself.

One man even urged the young men to "make many mistakes and fail many times" because learning and growth occur only in facing, thinking about and correcting mistakes and failures.

What wholesome wisdom can you share with your sons and grandsons, daughters and granddaughters?

Listen, children, to a father's instruction...that you may gain insight. (Proverbs 4:1)

Strengthen the bonds between grandfathers, fathers and sons, Son of God.

Giving Back

Deanna Slamans brings a personal perspective to her role as a houseparent at Pennsylvania's Milton Hershey School.

Slamans was once a resident at the school which provides free education and housing to at-risk children. It changed her life. She was seven when her mother committed suicide. Her father was absent, so she moved in with relatives in a dangerous neighborhood. At 13, Slamans went to Milton Hershey where she found a safe, loving home.

Now, with her husband, Andy, she makes a positive difference in the lives of troubled youngsters. "When you live with poverty, unhealthy relationships and injustice, you think that's all there is in the world," said Slamans, the mother of two.

Her family lives with 12 boys in a big on-campus house. Slamans finds it a hectic but rewarding life.

In giving, we receive, often in ways we might never imagine.

Give, and it will be given to you. (Luke 6:38)

People of every age yearn for the kindness I can share with them. Show me how to aid them, Merciful Lord.

Father and Son Savor Each Moment

Dana Jennings and his son, Owen, share similar interests in music and literature. More recently they have shared something far more profound: life-threatening illness.

Owen, an athlete and Dartmouth College student, had autoimmune liver failure. "Those first few days when Owen's liver failed were the absolute worst of my life," says Jennings.

Then, the elder Jennings learned that he himself had an aggressive form of prostate cancer. The bond between father and son took on a new and deeper dimension.

"We look at each other these days, and we are pierced by our mutual sense of mortality," says Jennings. Owen's liver has healed, though he's still on immuno-suppressants; and Jennings awaits the outcome of his prostate cancer treatments. Yet, their bond has forever deepened.

Trials can strengthen our capacity to love.

Cast your burden on the Lord, and He will sustain you. (Psalm 55:20)

Soothe those who worry, Gentle Savior.

All You Can Eat, But Perhaps Shouldn't

Many restaurants offer an "all you can eat" buffet. Whether at a food court or at a local eatery, consumption, sometimes to excess, is becoming the norm.

In U.S. Catholic magazine, writer Bryan Cones says the trend is spiritually precarious and that an over-consumption mentality is not only bad for people's health, but also strains Earth's resources.

"Much of the natural world has been pushed to fragility under the strain of so many hungry human mouths," writes Cones. He adds, "Nature is barely able to recover from our feeding," and "we humans are beginning to put locusts to shame."

He recommends a fasting which would "reveal just how dependent we are on our fellow creatures for survival."

Consume in moderation, and only what you actually need.

The distress of sleeplessness...nausea and colic are with the glutton. (Sirach 31:20)

Inspire us to fast from over eating and gluttony, Holy Wisdom.

A Thoughtful Good-bye

You may recall that there was a great deal of media coverage about the changes in NBC television's late night lineup awhile back.

When the network decided to return Jay Leno to the spot after the 11 o'clock news, Conan O'Brien who had hosted the *Tonight Show* for only a few months chose to leave. Lots of money and some nastiness were thrown around. But the night O'Brien said good-bye, he had a positive message:

"All I ask of you, especially young people is one thing. Please don't be cynical. I hate cynicism—it's my least favorite quality and it doesn't lead anywhere. Nobody in life gets exactly what they thought they were going to get. But if you work really hard and you're kind, amazing things will happen."

Well said. Work hard. Be kind. Stay positive. You never know what wonders God has in store.

The Lord's servant must not be quarrelsome but kindly to everyone. (2 Timothy 2:24)

Spirit of Hope, calm my heart and let me trust in You.

Young People and Mental Health

It isn't easy to be a young person these days.

Five times as many high school and college students are coping with anxiety or other mental health issues as those who lived during the 1930's. According to a study conducted by five universities, when comparing young people who took a particular psychological test in 1938 with those who took it in 2007, many of today's students revealed such problems as stress, depression and trouble with authority.

Moreover, UCLA's 2008 survey of college freshmen found that three-quarters of them said that it was "very important" or even "essential" to be financially well off. Experts say this attitude is likely to lead to distress and disillusionment.

Expectations from parents, teachers, coaches, peers, society—and from within—can create problems for today's youth. Guide the young people in your life along a more fulfilling path.

If God is for us, who is against us?
(Romans 8:31)

Father, grant me the confidence to seek Your will.

Lovin' Spoonful

Edwin Williams estimates that he has 600 designs for spoons. But this craftsman does not just carve ordinary spoons out of wood, but lovespoons, a centuries-long tradition in his native Wales.

Originally courting gifts, the lovespoon is today given for a variety of reasons, including friendship and birthdays. Williams, who has been carving since childhood, made his first lovespoon 30 years ago.

Some traditional elements are included in designs. Ships, for example, stand for a safe voyage through life; anchors mean finding a safe place to settle; a heart symbolizes love. Other symbols personalize the spoon for particular couples. Williams notes that the wooden creations last a lifetime, and are often passed down through generations of families.

What we create, in our minds and with our hands, can bring joy to others.

The Lord will fulfill His purpose for me; Your steadfast love, O Lord, endures forever. Do not forsake the work of Your hands. (Psalm 138:8)

The beauty of Your creation, Spirit of God, inspires me, and gives me hope.

Health Benefits From Optimism?

Optimistic women may derive health benefits such as a lower risk of heart disease because of their outlook.

"Taking into account income, education, healthy behaviors like controlling blood pressure and whether or not you are physically active, whether or not you drink or smoke, we still see optimists with a decreased risk of death compared to pessimists," notes Dr. Hilary Tindle, lead author of an academic research study, quoted in Time magazine.

The reasons aren't entirely clear and more research is needed, but it's possible that optimistic people have more friends and a larger social network for support. They might also be able to manage stress better because of their physiological makeup.

Positive attitudes can have a ripple effect. Develop your own sunny outlook and urge those dear to you to do the same.

Your life will be brighter than the noonday; its darkness will be like the morning. (Job 11:18)

Savior, open my heart to Your joy each day.

Keeping Christmas Year 'Round

You can keep Christmas alive for 365 days according to *Liguorian* magazine. Try these ideas:

- See God in yourself. "The Word became flesh" says the Gospel according to John. How well do you treat your body and your soul?

- See God in all people. Genesis says, "God created humankind in His image." To mistreat a human being is to desecrate the image of God in that person.

- See God in every living creature. All creatures have value and dignity, regardless of how they might be useful to us. Live so that all may flourish.

- Be a sacrament of God's love. Affirm, enrich and strengthen yourself, your spouse, family, friends, and strangers.

Live the joy of Christ's birth each day.

Love your neighbor as yourself. (Mark 12:31)

Help me live Christmas all year long, Jesus, Infant of Bethlehem.

Never Give Up

When primatologist and conservationist Jane Goodall was 10 years old, she dreamed of going to Africa. Everyone laughed at her aspirations. As Goodall puts it, "My family had no money, Africa was far away and dangerous, and most of all, I was a mere girl."

Goodall was fortunate to have a mother who saw things differently. "My mother said, 'If you really want something and you work hard and take advantage of opportunities, and you never, ever give up, you will find a way.'"

As a young woman Goodall worked as a waitress to save enough to visit a friend in Kenya, and the rest is history. Goodall remains one of the world's most recognizable, well-known champions of animals and the environment today.

Keep a watchful eye for sexism, racism, and any other prejudices—and work to eradicate them.

He would speak of animals, and birds, and reptiles, and fish. People came from all the nations to hear the wisdom of Solomon. (1 Kings 4:33-34)

Gracious Father, remind Your children to respect one another and all Your creation.

Plant the Seed of Innovation

Unmanageable Internet files; information databases located in different countries; burdensome ordering systems—these are a few of the obstacles to sharing knowledge.

That's why a six-member team known as Science Commons was created to brainstorm legal and technical ways to combat these roadblocks to sharing original work.

The mission of Science Commons is crucial: Scientific data, findings, and resources need to be more widely available in order to spark discovery and innovation. Technological and human roadblocks must be understood and overcome. John Wilbanks, the executive director of Science Commons, states, "We have a network of knowledge. We need to liberate it enough that it can actually take off."

Share your wealth of knowledge with others. Yours could be the seed of an awe-inspiring discovery.

The tongue of the wise dispenses knowledge. (Proverbs 15:2)

Aid those working to make information sharing easier, Eternal God.

Words of Wisdom from Thoreau

Nineteenth century philosopher Henry David Thoreau had a keen appreciation of life. Here are some thoughts from *Thoreau and the Art of Life* worth considering.

A spiritual life is one of calmness, openness to mystery and openness to beauty. Remember that God is in the sheer silence. Augustine called God, "beauty ever ancient, ever new."

If you would have a quality life live simply; do unrushed, quality work. Avoid waste; live below your means. Allot a substantial portion of time for leisure and silence; live and work thoughtfully.

Joy is found in knowing who you are. Live this knowledge. Befriend yourself. Good health and life are temporary.

Begin now to live a spiritual, quality, joy-filled life.

Remember your Creator in the days of your youth, before the days...when you will say, "I have no pleasure in them." (Ecclesiastes 12:1)

Guide my living, Holy Spirit.

Stories Behind the Strawberries

Every morning on the way to his Manhattan office, Ray would stop at the corner fruit vendor. No matter the weather, Marcus was always there, pointing out the best choices to his customers.

As time passed, the two men started to share news of their families. Ray proudly told of his son's graduation from high school. Marcus said that he had put four children through high school and college with the income from the fruit stand. The two also chatted with other regulars.

Marcus' fruit stand soon became a spot for more than just selecting oranges or bananas or strawberries. It became a meeting place.

Everyone has a story to share. Sometimes, you've just got to stop, and check out the details.

Pay attention to how you listen. (Luke 8:18)

Show me, loving Father, how to hear Your children, my siblings.

Sure Ways to Feel Good

Looking for a way to make a difference? Here's a sampling of suggestions from *AARP Magazine:*

- Make a soldier smile. Send upbeat letters or gifts to members of the U.S. Armed Services.

- Get in the kitchen and cook. Help low-income families learn to cook more nutritious meals.

- Protect a national treasure. Work to preserve one of the nearly 400 parks and historical sites run by the National Park Service.

- Inspire a youngster. Offer the benefit of your expertise and open minds to career possibilities.

- Welcome a refugee. Help someone feel at home here. Lend a hand to get a life that's known turmoil on a new track.

And, with every task, offer a prayer—to give thanks for God's abiding presence in all we do.

I declare what I have seen in the Father's presence; as for you, you should do what you have heard from the Father. (John 8:38)

My Lord, stay with me. Give me hope.

O Canada

Every July 1st, Canadians celebrate Canada Day, which commemorates the union in 1867 of the British North American provinces into a single nation. In a *New York Times* article several Canadians living in the United States discussed what they miss most about home.

Melissa Auf der Maur explains, "It's the Canadian mosaic, which is fundamentally different from the American melting pot, that I treasure most. That mosaic makes the coexistence of Francophone and Anglophone cultures possible."

Lisa Naftolin states, "I miss the 'u' in color."

Sarah McNally declares, "I miss the winter sun on snow and ice, the blue sky too cold for a scrap of cloud. My expatriate sorrow is that the weather has become warmer."

Don't forget where you and your family come from. Celebrate the richness of your history and culture.

Paul...addressed them..."I am a Jew, born in Tarsus in Cilicia, but brought up in (Jerusalem) at the feet of Gamaliel. (Acts 21:40,22:3)

Adonai, help me be proud of my family's roots.

"Staycation" Suggestions

Here are some ideas for a week's "staycation"—a vacation without really leaving home.

Monday: Be a tourist in your own city. Book a bus tour or a guided walking tour, or just buy a good walking map.

Tuesday: Browse museums, art galleries, historic landmarks.

Wednesday: Host a dinner party for old friends.

Thursday: Pack those leftovers from yesterday, a good book, a blanket, insect spray and sun block and spend a day in the park.

Friday: Sleep late. Get a massage or manicure. Nap.

Saturday: Browse green markets, antique fairs, yard sales. Treat yourself to lunch in a new restaurant.

Sunday: Worship. Enjoy brunch with loved ones. Then relax and savor the vacation you've just enjoyed.

There is nothing better for (workers) than to be happy and enjoy themselves.
(Ecclesiastes 3:12)

Help us find enjoyment close to home, God.

Surgeons Helping Soldiers

Army Staff Sgt. Jeff Colpetzer remembers the day that changed his life forever. "It was just a regular day in the marketplace" in Iraq, says Colpetzer. While on foot patrol he was hit by a shoulder-fired rocket that grazed his face, pulverizing much of the bone and severing a cranial nerve.

Doctors saved his life, but couldn't do much about the way he looked. Because thousands of soldiers have been severely injured in the Iraq war, in some cases it can be years before they have surgery to improve their appearance.

But a group of plastic surgeons donate their time and skills to Iraq Star, an organization that links surgeons to soldiers who need cosmetic surgery. The surgeons have improved the appearance of nearly 50 soldiers to date.

"He gave me my smile back," says Colpetzer of the surgeon who helped him.

How can the gift of your skills help others?

It is well with those who deal generously. (Psalm 112:5)

Give us a spirit of generosity, Prince of Peace.

Forgotten Heroes

After Edwin Burrows read a brief account of British prisons for captured colonial soldiers during the American Revolution, he wanted to learn more. His search for books on the subject was unsuccessful. So, after extensive research on his own, Burrows wrote *Forgotten Patriots: The Untold Story of American Prisoners During the Revolutionary War.*

The book focuses on New York City, where the British imprisoned about 30,000 Americans (of whom 18,000 died). It describes their environment: damp prison ships or old warehouses with deliberate neglect, "brutal whippings, rancid food, and cramped conditions common."

As Burrows says, "our own experience with prisoner abuse led us to believe that we are supposed to do better."

Learn from yesterday's heroes. Do what you can to make our nation worthy of their sacrifices.

Taking account of the resurrection...he made atonement for the dead.
(2 Maccabees 12:43,45)

Redeemer, preserve our liberties for which men and women of every age have paid the last full measure of devotion.

Harvesting Bounty for the Needy

Seventeen-year old Melissa Monette realizes that when people think of her native state, Hawaii, they usually think of lush, beautiful tropics, as well as wealth and leisure. Monette, however, knows of a different Hawaii—one of poverty and financial hardship for many.

She experienced this firsthand when her own beloved grandmother, a widow, couldn't make ends meet on her income. In response, Monette founded A Harvest for Many, a program that redirects the bounty of her picturesque home state to those in need.

The program recruits store owners and individuals to donate fruit and fresh vegetables to those in need. Moreover, it offers nutrition and exercise classes to more than a hundred older people on a regular basis.

Look around you and see who could use a helping hand.

Do not store up for yourselves treasures on earth...but store up for yourselves treasures in heaven. (Matthew 6:19-20)

Enlighten us in ways to share Your riches, Creator.

Share the Wealth

Successful businessman Frank Buonanotte was fascinated by a History Channel documentary about firefighters. Though it's impossible to see through smoke, the film explained that thermal imaging helps firefighters identify colleagues and victims. Yet many fire stations can't afford these special cameras.

After corresponding with the National Fallen Firefighters Foundation, Buonanotte set up a nonprofit called 500 for Life. It has donated 40 cameras to fire departments across 25 states since it was established in 2007. Buonanotte is happy for the success of his charity, and he also feels more fulfilled as a person. "I've been able to help firefighters save more lives. It doesn't get any better than that," he says.

Financial wealth is not meant to be hoarded, but used to serve our brothers and sisters.

Those who...are rich...are to do good, to be rich in good works, generous, and ready to share. (1 Timothy 6:17,18)

Inspire each one of us to generosity, Holy Spirit.

Tea and Jam for Change

A church group in Cutler Bay, Florida, hardly seems the place to find "radicals." But the gift baskets put together by parishioners at Our Lady of the Holy Rosary Catholic Church in that city—an assortment of teas, jam and chocolate – could challenge what we think of as business as usual.

Church groups across the country are building awareness among consumers of the effect of their choices, while standing in solidarity with small farmers and skilled artisans in the United States and around the world.

For example, many of us don't realize that an $8 can of coffee trickles down just 30 cents for the farmer. With fair trade products, that's not the case; the farmer earns more, since there's a more direct connection between consumer and producer.

God's love binds us in this one human family. That's why the plight of our neighbors becomes our own.

When you give a banquet, invite the poor...and you will be blessed. (Luke 14:13-14)

Bless the work of my hands, Master, the fruit of my labor.

A Jar of Memories

Annie and her daughter Elizabeth had been having trouble connecting. The preteen was involved with numerous school activities and even community theater. Annie's work schedule left little room for anything except collapsing into bed at the end of a long day.

Then early one Saturday morning, the two awoke at the same time. "Let's go for a walk on the beach," Elizabeth suggested to her mother. The two set off, walking the short distance from their home to the shore. There they gathered shells, laughing and enjoying the sunshine.

On the way back, mother and daughter stopped in a thrift store where Annie bought a glass jar for their shell collection. Elizabeth added a note that read, "Mom and me, beach visit," and the date.

Memories of loving times with family and friends are to be treasured—tucked away in our mind for comfort on difficult days.

You have made known to me the ways of life; You will make me full of gladness with Your presence. (Acts 2:28)

Help me, Lord, to see Your loving presence around me.

A Tough Tradition

Every year in Scotland, longstanding tradition is honored when brawny, burly men meet for the Braemar Gathering, a part of the Highland Games.

At the Gathering, tartan-kilted men demonstrate their strength and grit by competing in caber (beam) tossing, hammer throwing and the daunting Long Leap. These echo the practices of their Scottish ancestors and were begun as early as 1044 to identify the fastest and strongest warriors for battle.

By the 1800s the Braemar Gatherings took on a more festive character, although the grueling competitive games and superhuman strength still remain part of the tradition.

What are your family's traditions? What's your history? Talk with older relatives and treasure your past.

Keep My teachings as the apple of your eye... write them on...your heart. (Proverbs 7:2-3)

Help me hold fast to Your Word, Divine Master.

Think about Not Thinking

Have you ever tried to meditate? Many believe that meditation is a difficult practice meant to achieve a mysterious, altered state of mind. But meditation does not aim at an altered state nor is it difficult.

There are two kinds of thoughts: those that suddenly pop into your head and are the traces of previous thoughts and experiences in the neural pathways of your brain; and thoughts that occur in streams, which you latch onto and tend to follow naturally.

What, then, is the best way to meditate? Sit comfortably. Practice ignoring the first kind of thought and letting go of the second. Elongate the spaces between your thoughts and just stop thinking about thinking.

The relaxation and peace of meditation will recharge your energy and focus. Enjoy the peace that comes from God.

Be still, and know that I am God! (Psalm 46:10)

Help us enter into still silence, Holy Wisdom.

Tailor for the Train

For two decades, employees of New York's Metro-North Railroad went to Joseph Cirillo, the commuter train line's in-house tailor.

Cirillo helped Metro-North conductors and station agents look their best until his retirement in the summer of 2009. From his office in Grand Central station he did everything from custom-fitting uniform jackets (which have ten pockets) to fixing buttons and repairing hems to designing maternity uniforms for the railroad's employees.

Cirillo began his career in Italy, in an uncle's tailor shop. By 13, he was making pants from scratch. As much as his tailoring skills, train personnel counted on Cirillo's advice. "They enjoy looking good," he said.

Each day the people in our lives count on our loving, skillful actions. Make your work count.

Their clothing is...the product of skilled workers. (Jeremiah 10:9)

Help us, Lord, respect the intelligence, artistry and skill of crafts persons and all who use their hands and hearts to serve others.

Fighting Terrorism

After Greg Mortenson's youngest sister died in 1993, he pledged to leave her favorite necklace on Pakistan's K2, the second highest mountain in the world. He failed when he got lost on a glacier.

But he found a new mission while recuperating in a village called Korphe. Watching the 82 village children writing in the sand with sticks, Mortenson promised to help build them a proper school for all the boy and girls.

A few years later, Mortenson founded the Central Asia Institute (CAI), which has built 91 schools in Pakistan and 39 in Afghanistan. Educating these children combats terrorism by reducing poverty and ignorance. Meanwhile, Mortenson continues to promote peaceful relations with Muslim communities.

Failure always comes with a chance for success. Jump at the opportunities before you to improve the welfare of others.

Whoever does the will of God is My brother and sister and mother. (Mark 3:35)

Show us, Holy Wisdom, how we can help children and their parents, especially those who are unemployed, homeless or hungry.

Living without Meat

A vegetarian lifestyle can be challenging. David Noonan, who is relatively new to vegetarianism, finds that, "it's a lot easier to grow a belly than to not grow one."

But for health reasons he decided to go vegan (no animal products) and after two months had lost 12 pounds. Having to plan every meal and snack can be demanding, but worth it.

If you're thinking about becoming a vegetarian or vegan , here are some suggestions:

- Eat healthily, being sure to get enough protein.
- Try meat product substitutes in your favorite recipes.
- Download vegetarian or vegan recipes from the internet and buy a cookbook that specializes on this fare and start cooking.

Caring for your health means working at it day by day.

Do not eat without restraint; for overeating brings sickness. (Sirach 37:29-30)

Whether or not we choose to refrain from eating animal products, Lord of life, remind us to eat so as to preserve our health.

A Note in the Mail

Teresa's usual work stress—writing deadline on top of writing deadline—was compounded by an escalating family squabble. On this day, there seemed to be a large dark cloud looming over her world.

But then the morning mail arrived, bringing a letter from a reader of the magazine Teresa edited. The letter writer praised the publication, and Teresa's column, in particular. "I so look forward to receiving the magazine," the note concluded. "I just wanted to write to encourage you in your efforts."

Teresa placed the note, complete with its cover image of a bright yellow sunflower, on the shelf above her desk. Every day, especially the difficult ones, it would remind her of the light always trying to peek through the darkness.

Take a moment today to encourage someone—to be that ray of hope in their difficult times.

I would encourage you with my mouth, and the solace of my lips would assuage your pain. (Job 16:5)

You are my light and my hope, Lord. Guide me.

The Thrill of Victory

Just because you can't dunk a basketball, hit a home run or dance with the stars doesn't mean you can't become an accomplished competitor and savor the thrill of victory. *USA Weekend* described some contests where people display skill even if they're not elite athletes.

Graham Walker, 42, co-founder of the World Rock Paper Scissors Society says anyone can "walk in as a nobody and walk out as a champion." Still, the most successful will be skilled at reading body language and noticing patterns. "You're dealing with two people who have to make decisions on each throw."

In the U.S. Air Guitar Championships, performers strum their nonexistent guitars before live audiences. Special musical talent isn't needed, but winners have to keep at it for 60-second intervals and persuade audiences they really "feel" the music.

Use your interests and talents to do good—and to enjoy yourself as well.

I speak these things...so that they may have My joy made complete in themselves. (John 17:13)

Divine Master, may I rejoice in Your goodness and Your glory and strive to imitate Your joy.

Recipe for Leadership

Countless articles opine on what makes a person a real leader. Is it charisma? An ability to connect to others?

According to Randy Marsh, who has umpired five World Series, the answer is none of the above. He believes great managers are leaders who know when to ask for help; prepare exhaustively for their jobs; and do their homework.

Marsh stresses that what makes an ordinary manager a great manager is the strength to make unpopular decisions, provided they are backed by honest, well-meaning conviction and a strong basis in furthering the business at hand. He adds that great managers—and leaders—develop the confidence to make on-the-spot decisions through preparation and attention to details.

What qualities do you admire in others? Make it a point to compliment a job well done. A kind word can go a long way.

Pleasant speech multiplies friends. (Sirach 6:5)

Help me speak kindly to others, Precious Savior.

A Summer Seat

It's the summer seat of choice—the Adirondack chair.

Defined as "an outdoor armchair having an angled back and seat made of wide, usually wooden slats," it was the creation of Thomas Lee in 1903. The Boston blueblood nailed together the first such chair at his family's summer house in Westport, New York. Then, according to his niece, he got family members to test different seat angles to settle on the right fit and design.

The chair's broad arms are perhaps its best feature—wide enough for a cup of coffee and a newspaper, or a sandwich, soft drink and book, with ample room leftover for your forearms and elbows. For that reason, one writer described Lee's creation as "a one-person resort you put in your yard."

The inventions of others can fill our lives with joy and lessen our burdens.

He raises up the poor...He lifts the needy...to make them sit with princes and inherit a seat of honor. (1 Samuel 2:8)

I give thanks for the gifts of Your creation, Master.

Guardian Angels

To them, he was "papa." The poor living near Mary Help of Christians parish in Sirsiya in southeastern Nepal came to depend on their beloved priest, Father John Prakash Moyalan.

So his murder one July morning in 2008 was painful for many. Armed men had forced their way into the house Father John shared with the other parish priest, Father Jacob, demanding money from Father John. He refused and was shot to death.

Instead of seeking vengeance the villagers forgave the murderous robbers. Many even took time off from their farm work to stand guard and protect their remaining priest from harm.

Our own life's witness should offer others an example of God's selfless love and compassion.

Fear the Lord and revere His priests. (Sirach 7:29)

My life is Yours, Creator. Inspire me to serve others.

Life-Changing Journey

One trip is all it took. Linda Gilbert and a friend journeyed to Honduras as part of a service initiative. She returned home to Vermont wondering how much more they could do for the poor of this Central American country.

So Gilbert, along with family, friends and neighbors whom she encouraged, reached out to Hands to Honduras-Tela. In one year 70 volunteers, ages 8 to 79, dug foundations, constructed classrooms, and conducted health screenings for hundreds of Tela residents. The Vermonters also brought generous amounts of donated goods.

"We brought a woman named Juanita a wheelchair," said Linda Gilbert's husband, Al. "She hadn't left her home, a three-walled shack, in three years."

Urgent needs surround us. All carry the same message: Action required.

God...will not overlook your work and the love that you showed for His sake. (Hebrews 6:10)

We pray for Your Spirit to surround us, compassionate Lord, refreshing our lives.

Need a Volunteer? Just Ask

Do you know that the number one reason people don't volunteer is because they are not asked?

According to Susan Stern, chair of a national commission on community service and a volunteer herself, most volunteers get started because someone simply asked them for their time or involvement.

"Volunteers can be a powerful resource and a major conduit for change," says another expert on the subject.

Another reason compelling some volunteers is gratitude. Jim Mitchell, a retired auditor who volunteers for the elderly, says that his own financial security moved him to work to help others have the same. "That's really the reason I got involved," he says.

God's spirit dwells in each of us. Allow it to shine through with works of charity for your neighbors.

> **Clothe yourselves with compassion, kindness, humility, meekness, and patience. (Colossians 3:12)**

> *Merciful God, keep me mindful that each and every one of us is called to give, to love, to serve.*

Today's Logo Is...

It has celebrated the birthdays of artist Norman Rockwell and composer Giuseppe Verdi, as well as the cartoonist who created Popeye the Sailor Man. It marks holidays and historical events—the fall of the Berlin Wall, for example—and moments from pop culture, such as the day Sesame Street first aired on television. More often, it has just been itself, nothing special about it at all.

"It" is the logo for Google, the Internet's premier search engine. Artists have created "doodles" to commemorate various anniversaries and events, always weaving the art to spell out the site's signature name.

Like Google, some days remind us of extraordinary events, in our own lives and in the world around us. And then other days pass by uneventfully. Every day, though, we give thanks for the gift of life and the love of those around us.

Today you have ordained yourselves for the service of the Lord...and so have brought a blessing on yourselves. (Exodus 32:29)

Send me a sign, Lord, to help me know Your will.

A Helping Hand in Prison

Almost one-third of inmates in U.S. prisons are over fifty. More than 3,000 prisoners die of natural causes every year. With this aging population, about 75 prisons have started hospice programs.

The volunteers are prisoners themselves. They feed the dying, take them to the bathroom, talk to them, even hold their hands at the end. Kathleen Allan, director of nursing at New York's Coxsackie Correctional Facility, believes these volunteers have "a desire to redeem themselves, so even when it gets hard they're able to plow through it."

An inmate volunteer said, "I've come to identify with these guys, not because we're inmates, but because we're human beings. What they're going through, I'll go through."

Every one of us who knows life will know death. Grow in respect for the lives of all God's children.

Do not rejoice over any one's death; remember that we must all die. (Sirach 8:7)

Help me to love those who are hard to love with Your love;, to forgive the unforgivable with Your forgiveness, Savior.

Invisible Do-Not-Hire Lists?

It pays for job hunters to be aware of possible pitfalls so they don't inadvertently trip up their own job search.

A *Wall Street Journal* story mentions some areas of concern. Recruiters mainly want to weed out "liars, losers and misfits." But an applicant might also be blacklisted for exaggerating qualifications or making silly jokes not seen as funny in an interview.

Even if they don't admit it, hiring managers often keep unofficial tallies of undesirable applicants. There are also career dangers in posting inappropriate or inaccurate information on social media sites such as Facebook. One recruiter lost interest in a candidate who "represented herself in a way that would not align with the company's philosophy and ethics."

On-line or in person, maintain your values and make a positive impression.

Righteous lips are the delight of a king, and he loves those who speak what is right. (Proverbs 16:13)

Guide me in always being truthful and honorable, Paraclete.

Sharing Soles...

In 1999, Chicago hairdresser Mona Purdy saw Central American children tarring their bare soles so they could run a race. An American orthopedic surgeon told her that he regularly amputated infected feet and legs. Purdy also learned that shoes were a prerequisite for school. Once home Purdy asked for donations of children's shoes for an orphanage.

A decade later, Share Your Soles, a not-for-profit begun by Purdy, collects elegant sandals, hiking boots, gym shoes and baby shoes in a 400,000 square-foot Alsip, Illinois, warehouse. They're sanitized, sorted, and polished by volunteers. Those that have holes, tears or excessive wear are discarded. In a decade 900,000 pairs of shoes have been distributed around the world.

Use your imagination to help those who lack the basics.

I was naked and you gave Me clothing. (Matthew 25:36)

Holy Trinity, inspire my volunteering on behalf of my needy sisters and brothers.

Laid Off and Losing Weight

Editor Michael Johansson logged 60-hour workweeks, devoting little care to his own health. Then the economic downturn caused him to lose his job—and shift his focus. He slowed down, started making better food choices, and exercised. The result: Johansson lost weight and felt better.

With the surge in unemployment in recent years, researchers have begun to look more closely at the link between joblessness and overall good health. Some see the connection rooted in the fact that the unemployed finally had time to relax and focus on themselves, even with the stress of looking for work.

But that doesn't mean that those still on the job can't make their health a priority. In fact, their daily tasks should include time to exercise, eat right, and take short breaks during the workday.

What we do for a living is important, but so is how we treat others and ourselves.

Oh, restore me to health and make me live! (Isaiah 38:16)

Protect me, Father; strengthen and keep me from harm.

Touching Moments

Infants need to experience human touch to thrive, but that's also true for adults. *The Mayo Clinic Health Letter* suggests some ways to enhance the sense of touch in your own life:

- Get massages regularly. They can improve your immune system and decrease pain and stiffness.

- Get a manicure or pedicure, even regular hair care. These are simple forms of touch available to almost anyone.

- Join a ballroom dance group. It's good for your social life and for exercise.

- Get a pet. Companion animals provide physical closeness and unconditional acceptance. Plus they need your care and attention.

And don't forget to hug someone near and dear to you—it's good for both of you.

Jesus stretched out His hand and touched him. (Mark 1:41)

Jesus, Son of God and Son of Man, help me reach out to others—and to myself—in friendship and kindness.

Baked Ziti for 120

Brenden Gobell has had the same routine every other month since he was 12 years old. He, and his mom and sister, shop, cook and feed 120 people at a homeless shelter near their Connecticut home just as they have for eight years.

Complex issues have pushed these people onto the streets: mental illness, substance abuse, and unemployment, among them. Dinner is a high point of their day, and Gobell makes sure that he serves up healthy portions of respect and kindness, along with every delicious plate of pasta, salad, bread and cookies.

What started as assisting his mom has become an ongoing commitment for the young man. He fundraises to pay for the dinner ingredients and to provide linens and toiletries for the shelter.

Each of us can do our part to show love for our neighbor. The call to help is answered one need at a time.

Jesus said...“Feed My sheep.” (John 21:17)

As You share Your abundant love, Redeemer, so may I share my blessings with others.

Zoo Blues

Passengers on the Bronx Zoo's Skyfari gondola ride felt like the ones behind the glass when the gondolas unexpectedly stopped. Due to a malfunctioning gondola wheel, thirty-seven people were stuck in the air for up to five hours.

Being trapped in the cramped cars, "felt like a cage," one woman said. Another said she felt powerless, and thought the animals received better treatment than she did. A man said it was "a horrible thing—let's have room to roam, for people too."

The managing director of an African gorilla project, Richard Carroll, said it was a good lesson. "Humanity needs to learn humility. We're not masters of the universe. We're part of the natural world."

Let's develop a healthy humility as part of God's creation and as His children.

For freedom Christ has set us free. ...Do not submit again to a yoke of slavery. (Galatians 5:1)

Remind us, Spirit of Understanding, to give ourselves and others the freedom to live the lives You laid out for us.

Going Home Again Via Computer?

Novelist Thomas Wolfe famously wrote that "You can't go home again," because the past is, well, over.

But has technology made it possible to "go home again?" The Internet and its plethora of social networking sites, map viewers, blogs and chat rooms have fueled a near epidemic of people trying to reconnect with their past. Some try to view their childhood homes on map programs, while others scour the Net to find long-lost friends or loved ones.

According to one writer, such a journey can result in disappointment. For example, revisiting your childhood home may fall short of the images and memories you hold from your youth.

Are memories best left as memories? Or is technology a boon to keeping us connected to our personal history? Perhaps, like many things, it's a bit of both.

**But I trust in You, O Lord; I say, "You are my God." My times are in Your hand.
(Psalm 31:14-15)**

Jesus, walk with me on this journey we call life.

Tea, Chips and a Sandwich Go a Long Way

Peter Blake has a mission. He's one of a group of amateur pilots who donate their flying skills, planes and fuel for medical missions.

"Our passengers are going through traumatic events and feel weak and ill," says Blake, who owns a heating and air conditioning business. "Snapple, chips and a turkey sandwich for everyone. Even when you don't feel well, most people can handle a simple turkey sandwich."

Angel Flight originated in Georgia in 1983 to fly people with medical problems to and from treatments in distant cities; Blake's Northeast chapter has flown more than 38,000 missions, transporting more than 54,000 patients and family members.

"After some flights I cry on my way home," Blake admits. "It makes you realize how lucky we are, that we don't have to deal with what these families do."

What a blessing to help others in their time of need!

I will comfort you. (Isaiah 66:13)

Deliver us from evil, Father; save us from suffering.

A Fighting Chance

Around the world, estimates put the number of "child soldiers" at some 300,000.

Alusine was one of them. He was only 9 when he was dragged off at gunpoint, and forced to be one of the "little killers" in the civil war of his homeland, Sierra Leone. Eventually he escaped and found his way to a Catholic camp where he and dozens of other young people were offered hope for a new life.

"Many of these boys were taken from their families at a very young age and have known nothing but war," says one missionary who served in that camp. "We try to give them a home, a family, a reminder of God's ceaseless love."

So many people need to be reminded that God's love gives us all a fighting chance.

By day the Lord commands his steadfast love, and at night His song is with me. (Psalm 42:8)

Every day, may I remember Your command, Lord, to love my neighbor.

Wisdom Keeper

Canadian novelist Margaret Atwood participated in a video series that made her rethink her role as an "elder" in society. The series, called Wisdom Keepers, consists of interviews with successful older people. Its purpose: to motivate young adults.

At first, Atwood felt that she wasn't any wiser than when she had been 20. In fact, she admitted that she felt pressured to give good advice, but felt unequal to the task.

Then Atwood remembered what she had been told about Inuit elders: "An Elder knows what to do in times of difficulty...by having endured hard times before." Atwood realized that she and her peers have an obligation to share their experiences with youth.

Each of us should listen to others with respect and courtesy—and not be afraid to share our own wisdom.

How attractive is sound judgment in the gray-haired, and for the aged to possess good counsel! (Sirach 25:4)

Inspire old and young to listen attentively to one another, Ancient of Days.

Reach for the Stars

Have you ever wanted to get a closer look at the stars? What about those moons of Earth and Jupiter and the rings around Saturn? Howard Sims can see these—and more—through the 300-pound telescope he built at his home in Madison County, Georgia.

As a boy, Sims spent many nights sprawled across the grass gazing at the sky. "All my life, most anything I saw I could make," he says. With this positive attitude, Sims set out to quench his childhood curiosity by building an 18-foot-tall observatory. Proud of his work, he shares his home observatory with many schoolchildren and other visitors.

Passion, hard work, and courage result in success. Find your passion, cultivate it, and don't be afraid of any obstacles.

The stars shone in their watches and were glad; He called them, and they said, "Here we are!" They shone with gladness for Him who made them. (Baruch 3:34)

Bless us with courage and perseverance, Holy Wisdom.

Your Best Walking Partner

It's time for a walk. Whether the sky is blue or gray; whether it's rainy and windy, or hot and sticky, who will be your companion? How about your dog—who will neither try to get out of going along nor try to convince you to stay home?

The University of Missouri studied 54 seniors in an assisted living home. The 12 who walked a dog from a local animal shelter had a 28 percent improvement in walking speed. They were more consistent in walking daily. Of those who used canes or walkers, many stopped using them, saying, "I'm physically fit enough to take my dog for a walk." In fact, as they arrived at the animal shelter they eagerly asked, "Where's my dog?"

Every day is a good day for a walk. Find an encouraging partner—human or canine.

When the people of Nineveh saw (Tobit) walking along in full vigor and with no one leading him, they were amazed. (Tobit 11:16)

Thank you, Lord and Creator, for our companion animals.

The Statue of Liberty and the Farm

By July, the three-acre Governors Island farm produces squash, tomatoes, eggplants and ground-cherries (relatives of gooseberries) while the Statue of Liberty gazes on.

One of a small handful of commercial organic farms in New York City, it produces tens of thousands of dollars of organic produce each year. This income provides stipends for teenagers who work there and at another farm in Brooklyn's Red Hook section.

Kimberly Vargas started as one of those student-volunteers. She is now a staff member teaching young children about food production. "I like feeling connected to the land," she says.

Amazing things happen when we take time to experience the beauty and bounty of the nature all around us.

Lord, how manifold are Your works!...the earth is full of Your creatures. (Psalm 104:24)

Generous God, increase my appreciation for the food You have provided for us.

Ready to Go the Extra Mile?

Some volunteers put real sweat into their charitable efforts. Take Jesuit Father Matthew Ruhl, an avid cyclist. Father Ruhl regularly participates in Portland, Oregon's Cycling for Change Fun Ride.

But Father Ruhl wants to go that extra mile. He plans to cycle across the entire country from Seattle, Washington, to Key West, Florida, to raise awareness of Catholic Charities' efforts to cut poverty in the United States in half over the coming decade.

Father Ruhl has recruited others to join him, Catholics and non-Catholics alike. "We're inviting anyone interested in eradicating poverty," he says.

Poverty knows no boundaries. Do what you can to ease the suffering of the poor.

You lack one thing; go, sell what you own, and give the money to the poor, and you will have treasure in heaven; then come, follow Me. (Mark 10: 21)

Show us how to help the destitute, Jesus, our Messiah.

Good Stewards

People of all faiths wonder about their appropriate role as stewards of God's good earth—and all His creatures. However, in *America* magazine, Kate Blake notes that some worry "that concern for animals as a part of God's creation is akin to idolatry."

Blake says that taking interest and showing responsibility for "the just treatment of what the Creator has made doesn't displace the Creator." In fact, the Catholic Catechism says, "Use of the... resources of the universe cannot be divorced from respect for moral imperatives."

Blake reminds us that "we live within nature but not as master." And she quotes Pope John Paul II: "Since they are beings endowed with feeling and sensitive to pain, man is required to ensure that the use of the creatures is never attended by suffering or physical torture."

Improve your stewardship of God's creation and His creatures.

God made the wild animals...the cattle...and everything that creeps upon the ground. ...And God saw that it was good. (Genesis 1:25)

Inspire our stewardship of Your creatures, Creation, God.

Hooked on Helping

After Kohl Crecelius saw his athletic older brother crocheting, he tried the hobby, too. Soon his high school friends Travis Hartanov and Stewart Ramsey were hooked. The trio make all types of beanies and have dubbed themselves the Krochet Kids.

In college, all three decided to volunteer and offer their service in faraway places with non-profits during summer break. It was then Ramsey had the idea that their crocheting could change the world.

"Let's teach Ugandan women how to crochet," he suggested, seeing this as a way to help them as they struggled to survive after a 20-year civil war. And Krochet Kids International was born. Today, Ugandan women sell their crocheted creations to people around the world to provide for their families' needs, including the education of their children.

What simple things can you do to make a difference for someone near or far. Stay open to every possibility.

Help the poor for the Commandment's sake. (Sirach 29:9)

I pray for those in need, Lord. Inspire me to help them.

Capturing Images and Blueberries

For over two decades, photographer David Brooks Stess has been going from New York City to Maine for the blueberry harvest. He says the harvest "detoxifies" him.

Stess joins the field workers who work back-breaking hours hand raking and picking blueberries in the desolate barrens north of Columbia Falls, in Maine's coastal Washington County. Later in the day, he takes pictures, all in black and white, of the workers, their primitive lodgings, and their work. The photographer hopes to publish his documentary-style work within the next few years.

Getting out of our familiar surroundings and comfort zone is invigorating and, importantly, enlightening. Make it a habit to reach out to new people and to go to new places whenever possible. Interacting with different people in their milieu breaks down prejudices.

In passing judgment on another you condemn yourself. (Romans 2:1)

Son of God, open our eyes to what unites us including our shared humanity.

Removing Stones from the Heart

A wounded country. That's how Archbishop Edward Charles describes his Sierra Leone homeland. The litany of horror unleashed during a decades-long civil war seems unfathomable to most, from drugged child soldiers to mutilation and murder.

But this Catholic leader stresses the need to forgive. "We must carry Jesus in our hearts, and not a pebble of hatred or vengeance, since that pebble becomes a rock, a stumbling block on our God-given journey," he explains.

All of us struggle to forgive others. But opening your heart and mind to forgiveness, frees us from anger and pain, and lets God in. And with God, all things are possible.

Forgive us our debts, as we also have forgiven our debtors. (Matthew 6:12)

Merciful Father, help me to forgive even as I am forgiven.

Supersizing the "Care" in Care Packages

Annie Wignall was just 11 when she decided to ramp up the "care" aspect of the care packages for needy people.

Wignall helped found the Care Bags Foundation, to distribute care packages filled with useful, age- and gender-appropriate personal care items and toiletries to children in crisis who are forced to leave their homes abruptly. The foundation, run entirely by volunteers, fills more than 100 care bags monthly, which are distributed through children's services agencies and individuals across the country.

Says Wignall, "we cannot help everyone, but with each donor's help, we can make a difference, one Care Bag at a time, one child at a time."

No effort to help another human being is ever small. Every gesture of service and kindness matters.

**Clothe yourselves with compassion.
(Colossians 3:12)**

Gentle Savior, infuse us with compassion for one another.

Seeds For The Good-Food Revolution

Former pro basketball player Will Allen won a "genius grant" from the MacArthur Foundation for developing urban farming techniques and teaching youngsters to grow food in their neighborhoods.

Although he's a modest man, Allen recognizes the practical benefits of winning the much-publicized grant. "The thing that makes me happiest is that more people of color are joining the good-food revolution," said Allen, who adds, "It's about building sustainable food systems." He's the founder and chief executive of Growing Power, Inc. whose goal is to grow nutritious food everywhere there's need.

MacArthur recipients get annual $100,000 grants for five years with no spending restrictions. Allen earmarked some of his money for grants to at-risk college students thereby planting seeds of another kind.

Genius or not, each of us has the power to better our world.

To the present hour we are hungry and thirsty. ...We have become like the rubbish of the world, the dregs of all things. (1 Corinthians 4:13)

Blessed Trinity, show me how to assist those who hunger or thirst in my own community.

Hidden Value at Yard Sales

Richard Rubin, a big fan of yard sales, once bought a decades-old *Columbia Encyclopedia* which he described as heavy, obsolete, and not particularly attractive. So why did he buy it? Well, it cost $2 and he couldn't resist the bargain.

Yard sales are legendary bastions of trash and treasure. How any one item is characterized is often strictly in the eye of the beholder. Lots of people visit yard sales locally or when they travel. One multi-state sale has run along U.S. Highway 127 for 654 miles from Ohio to Alabama for a weekend every summer for over twenty years.

Of course, many folks host their own sales to clean out garages, basement and attics—and to pick up a few dollars in the process.

Something of value isn't always obvious, but we just may find it if we look hard enough.

Seek the things that are above, where Christ is. (Colossians 3:1)

Open my eyes to the true value of people and of things, Spirit of Wisdom.

Growing Debate

Which do you prefer: food that's organically grown or that's conventionally grown?

Most research confirms that higher-yielding modern variety crops generally have lower concentrations of nutrients. In addition, the healthiest soils produce the most nutritious food. And local or regional food systems lessen climate-changing carbon emissions, improve the health of the consumer, and increase economic development for the region by capturing more food dollars locally.

Still, conventionally grown produce tends to be cheaper and more easily attainable.

Served along with the facts in this food debate is a valuable lesson for living: Our decisions affect us—and others. Make your choices with that connection in mind.

They shall plant vineyards and drink their wine, and they shall make gardens and eat their fruit. (Amos 9:14)

Bless those who labor, Jesus of Nazareth.

The Unexpected Servant

When Michael Daube of New Jersey was finishing up his art degree at Brooklyn's Pratt Institute in 1988, he never imagined he'd end up serving the destitute with Mother Teresa.

Yet, that is exactly what happened to Daube. He described himself at that time as a "scraggly young American with a backpack" who was traveling in India shortly after completing college. A brief encounter with children begging in the streets led him face-to-face with Mother Teresa. She sent him to a rural town where medical supplies and treatment were desperately needed.

Within a year, Daube was back in India, raising money to build a 30-bed hospital. When people say that God works in mysterious ways, they are surely speaking the truth.

Where is God leading you?

Search me, O God, and know my heart...my thoughts...and lead me in the way everlasting. (Psalm 139:23,24)

Direct me, Divine Master, in the path of Your choosing.

Lord of the Dance

One day, while walking through the woods, Margaret Silf, author of *The Gift of Prayer*, noticed a withered dead leaf that seemed to be dancing in the breeze, held to a branch by an almost invisible spider's silk. She could not forget the image.

While speaking at a retreat, she mentioned the incident, tying it to "Jesus' parable of the vine … knowing that the true vine continually invites us into the freedom of the dance."

Later, one woman was moved to dance for joy after Mass. She told the others that several years earlier she'd been told to stop liturgical dancing and had given it up. Now she felt encouraged to praise God once more through dance.

Silf concluded that God knows "that when you are truly connected to the source of your being, you can dance freely and joyfully into the future, even in the shadow of a cross."

For freedom Christ has set us free. Stand firm ...do not submit again to a yoke of slavery. (Galatians 5:1)

Lord of the Dance, cure us of rigidity in thought and action.

There May Be Cash Around You

Stephanie Rabinowitz watched as auctioneers coaxed bidders to buy a vintage poster she had purchased years earlier in Paris. The piece, a stylish 1960 print by renowned French fashion illustrator Rene Gruau, fetched $425 that day. "I need the money to pay bills," explains Rabinowitz.

She's not alone. As the economic crisis has tightened its grip, people are finding that they need to raise cash to pay regular bills. One increasingly popular way to do this is to sell valuable items at auctions or online, such as through eBay.

Says one auction expert, "People don't always realize that they may have cash sitting on their bookshelves, or up on their walls."

Tough times call for creativity, and most of all, prayer. Pray for God's support when life's challenges become too big.

Let us therefore approach the throne of grace with boldness, so that we may receive mercy and find grace to help in time of need. (Hebrews 4:16)

Nothing shall separate us from love, Beloved of my Soul.

Eating and Thinking

At Food for Thought restaurant in Williamsburg, Virginia, some walls are adorned with images of great inventors like George Washington Carver, Eli Whitney and Alexander Graham Bell. Written on others and featured on a menu are thought-provoking philosophies such as this musing from Norman Vincent Peale: "Change your thoughts and you change your world."

Owner Howard Hopkins has created a tribute to great leaders, innovators, scientists, business people, and humanitarians—and a spot to share classic American dishes with family and friends.

"Only by tasting from the smorgasbord of knowledge, past and present, can we begin to satisfy our appetite for understanding," Hopkins says.

We need to satisfy our craving for all that's good and just.

Wisdom...says, "Come, eat of my bread and drink of the wine I have mixed...and walk in the way of insight." (Proverbs 9:1,4-5,6)

Holy Spirit, feed my body and soul, my mind and heart.

A Basketful of Hope

In the remote Amazon village of San Antonio de Pintuyacu, Peru, women skillfully weave fibers from the chambira palm tree into items for daily use. Among these are fishing nets, hammocks, purses, clothing and even dental floss.

Now this local craft has become a key element of Peru's economy. Women weave baskets for export to the United States. This is part of a larger effort to promote "productive conservation," allowing the rain forest to serve as a source of renewable economic resources while preserving its overall health and size.

Conservationists are fighting practices that exploit—and ultimately, destroy—the precious rainforest.

One Peruvian political leader says, "We are part of nature," and "when we destroy nature, we destroy ourselves."

That's a wise reminder for each of us, wherever we live.

God said, "Let...humankind...have dominion over... the earth. (Genesis 1:26)

Remind us that we are part of and stewards of Your creation, gracious Creator.

Chords of Salvation

Music has always been an important part of Elliott Glick's life. Growing up and struggling with his parents' divorce, Glick found peace—and a path out of the troubles many of his friends experienced—when playing his guitar and writing songs.

So when Glick, a father of four, saw some young people in his neighborhood looking lost and at risk, he spread the word about informal jam sessions at his local coffeehouse. Soon many afternoons there were filled with the teens' music.

"I know how quickly less positive influences can take over your life," Glick explains. "It was important to me to help kids stay focused. Music saved me, and I wanted to help others find that same solution."

What we value should be translated into our everyday relationships with one another—and always for the good of the community and the world around us.

Remember now, O Lord...how I have walked before You in faithfulness with a whole heart, and have done what is good in Your sight. (2 Kings 20:3)

Lead me from harm, Lord; shelter me in Your love.

Escape from the Normal

Have you ever wanted to escape the hustle and bustle of your city or town without leaving it entirely?

The High Line Park on Manhattan's West Side, which is built on an abandoned and reclaimed railroad line, is one such example. Hundreds of thousands of people have already flocked to the park. It's a place to relax, mingle with others, eat, and enjoy the city views. "Here people tend to be more friendly," a park-goer observed. Another said the park is "an incredible celebration of urban architecture."

In the midst of life's chaos, find a moment to sit and reflect or walk and admire the beauty of a park in your city or town.

From the...beauty of created things comes a corresponding perception of their Creator. (Wisdom of Solomon 13:5)

Help city dwellers find peace and beauty in their local parks, Holy God.

Unplanned Kindness

As their makeshift wheelchair ramp collapsed, a husband struggled to get his wife, who just had foot surgery, up the stairs into their home. A passing driver parked his truck and came to their rescue, carrying the woman inside. Then a woman—another stranger—stopped as well and returned later with a huge quantity of pot roast and potatoes—enough for three meals, in fact.

Then there's the pharmacist who dug in his pocket to find the few dollars a customer needed to fill her prescription. And a mother on her way home from work who helped a delivery person pick up all the packages that had just fallen from his hand truck onto the sidewalk.

All around us, every day, are opportunities to show kindness and love to our neighbors—even people we don't know. Act on your chance today!

If you keep My commandments, you will abide in My love. (John 15:10)

Compassionate Redeemer, we give thanks for Your boundless love and mercy.

Helping Parents Breathe

Imagine not understanding the dangers around you. That's the reality for Deborah Descenza's son Andrew, who is developmentally disabled due to a rare metabolic disorder. He thought nothing of walking in front of a moving car or playing with broken glass.

As Andrew grew, he became increasingly lonely, having to be isolated for his own protection. And Descenza grew exhausted by the nonstop attention he needed.

When her son turned 16, Descenza decided to do something for herself and parents in similar situations. She left her teaching post, raised money, and bought a farm in New Hampshire. There, young people like Andrew connect with the rhythm of the seasons and enjoy the satisfaction of completing a day's chores. And parents too got a break.

"When parents see their child flourish here," she says, "they can finally just breathe."

Burdens shared are burdens lightened.

Come to Me, all you that are weary and carrying heavy burdens, and I will give you rest. (Matthew 11:28)

I bring my worries and fears to You, Lord, for You are the source of all hope.

Words of Wisdom

What's the best advice you've ever gotten?

In a *Good Housekeeping* magazine article, famous and accomplished women shared the words that helped inspire their success.

For example, Madeleine Albright, the first woman U.S. Secretary of State, said that her father provided her with words of encouragement and a way to find confidence in tough situations. "Coming from Czechoslovakia, he sometimes mixed up English idioms," explains Albright. "He would say 'Strike it,' which was his version of 'Go for it.'" Albright says the phrase was her dad's way of telling her to "believe in myself and go after what I want."

Who gives you encouragement and instills confidence within you? Have you thanked them recently for such an invaluable gift?

I am sending him to you for this very purpose... to encourage your hearts. (Ephesians 6:22)

Let us remember to give thanks for all that You bestow upon us, Lord God.

Time for a Change?

Want to lower your risk of health problems such as heart disease? According to *Prevention Magazine*, research shows that with persistence these actions can make a real difference:

1. **Quit smoking**
2. **Eat more fruits and vegetables**
3. **Exercise regularly**
4. **Cut saturated fat**

Within 20 minutes of your last cigarette, your heart rate and blood pressure drop. Within 12 hours, toxic carbon monoxide in your blood decreases. Eventually lung function improves.

Try to eat five or more servings of fruits and vegetables daily by keeping your favorites handy. Eat whole grains, fish, poultry, and lean meat. Sharply limit saturated fats.

"The best exercise is the one you'll do," advises one expert. Whether you walk, cycle, dance or anything else—just get moving.

Commit to change and keep at it.

To those who by patiently doing good seek for glory and honor and immortality, He will give eternal life. (Romans 2:7)

It's hard to stick to good habits, Blessed Trinity. Help me to understand the value of persistence.

Living Independently

In the early 1980's, before the concept of assisted living became common, women in Rockville, Maryland, planned the state's first such facility for independent elders.

"Many elderly do not need the extensive and costly services of a nursing home," said Jean Brady, a parishioner at St. Mary's, one of the original planners. "Rather, they can maintain their independence with the benefit of some services such as housekeeping, meals and assistance with bathing, grooming, dressing and feeding."

In order to make the dream a reality, Brady needed skills. She learned about budgeting, grant writing, relevant laws, and how to collaborate with architects, government officials and others.

Victory Housing is now a $100-million dollar real-estate management and development nonprofit with a variety of housing for low and moderate-income residents.

Support elderly people in their desire to live safely and independently.

Praise the Lord...young men and women alike, old and young together! (Psalm 148:7,12)

Remind me to show respect to Your people, old and young, Spirit of Love.

Creating Art, Creating Meaning

Religion and art had always been inseparable to Marek Czarnecki as he grew up in Connecticut. Every morning, young Czarnecki would pray before the icon of Our Lady of Czestochowa. This icon was the only art in the house, which he shared with his Polish immigrant family. He also loved to read about and draw pictures of the saints. This interest blossomed into his dream of becoming an artist.

At a parish meeting years later, the new pastor asked why the Polish church Czarnecki and his family attended lacked an icon of Our Lady of Czestochowa. Czarnecki's father volunteered his son to paint the icon. Seeing people pray in front of it after it received a place of honor in the church, Czarnecki realized that nothing he had ever done was as meaningful as that work.

Czarnecki is now a successful iconographer. Achieve your dreams and inspire others along the way.

I have filled him with...ability, intelligence, and knowledge in every kind of craft, to devise artistic designs. (Exodus 31:3-4)

Lord and Creator, encourage those You have blessed with artistic gifts to use their talents well.

Life Threatening, Life Changing

Pediatric cancers are something most people don't want to talk about, let alone experience through a loved one's suffering.

To this day, Clint Beasley remembers how he felt when, as a first-time father, he learned that his then-10-month old son, Devin, had cancer. "It changed my life," says Beasley.

Devin has been cancer-free for nearly two years. But Beasley's life indeed changed as a result of the experience: he and other parents now lobby on Capitol Hill for increased funding for the treatment and cure of pediatric cancers.

At the same time, Beasley and his wife work to raise private funding for research—some $50,000 to $70,000 per year, through charitable events like golf tournaments and walk-a-thons.

How can you assist families undergoing the trauma of a loved one's major illness?

Physicians...pray to the Lord (for)...success in diagnosis and in healing. (Sirach 38:13-14)

Help me strive to end discrimination against survivors of cancer and other serious illnesses, Jesus.

Quest for the Lost

Andrew Carroll is on a scavenger hunt for lost places—like the spot on Manhattan's Fifth Avenue where Winston Churchill, crossing against the traffic light, was struck by a car in 1931 and nearly killed; or the hotel dining room in Washington, D.C. where poet Vachel Lindsay met a busboy named Langston Hughes who shared some poems with him and went on to become a great poet himself.

Carroll's Here Is Where campaign is—in the words of Keith Bellows, editor of *National Geographic Traveler*—"sensational." Bellows says, "He's peeling back a layer of history to expose Americans where they live and where they travel to things they otherwise might not have been aware of."

His hunt in 50 states is "just the kickoff," Carroll notes. "I'm going to be doing this for life," he adds.

All of life is a journey—filled with singular moments that teach, inspire and help make us strong.

The Lord...will send His angel with you and make your way successful. (Genesis 24:40)

I seek You, Father; reveal Your presence in this day.

Guitar Hero

When Les Paul died in 2009 at the age of 94, the world lost not only a virtuoso guitarist, but also an innovator and inventor.

Paul's passion for gadgetry developed early. At 10, he devised a harmonica holder from a coat hanger. Later, he experimented with guitar amplification and produced the first solid-body electric guitar. His recording studio advances created multi-track recording.

Saying often that he "didn't want to be an Edison," Paul simply said he invented things because he and others didn't have them. "I had no choice, really," he would say.

How creative are you? Do you make the best use of your God-given talent? If you do, it's good for you—and for your neighbors as well.

Let the favor of the Lord our God be upon us, and prosper for us the work of our hands. (Psalm 90:17)

May all I do, Master, bring harmony to Your creation.

Get Beyond Your Comfort Zone

Do you enjoy hearing or reading a wide range of opinions? Many men and women don't. They'd rather stick with people and sources that agree with their way of thinking.

Mohamed El-Erian, the chief executive officer of a global investment management firm, said in *Fortune* magazine that his father taught him differently. He told El-Erian, "Unless you read different points of view, your mind will eventually close, and you'll become a prisoner to a certain point of view that you'll never question."

Whatever issue concerns you, El-Erian believes, "There's a tendency for everyone to operate in a comfort zone and to want to read what is familiar to them. But if you are just used to following one person or one newspaper, you will miss big shifts."

Discover new perspectives. You needn't agree with others to learn from them.

Give me now wisdom and knowledge.
(2 Chronicles 1:10)

Holy Spirit, bless me with Your choicest gifts.

Say What?

Sometimes, despite the best of intentions, our words and attitudes lead to crossed signals, miscommunication and other snafus. Why? Mainly, it's because people relate through different communication styles and, as a result, end up with missed or mixed messages, hurt feelings and even conflict.

Figure out which communication style most resembles yours:

Assertive — Direct, clear and confident, this style lacks hidden meanings and subtlety.

Aggressive — A sometimes pushy and goal-oriented manner of communicating, this style uses persistence and force to get a point across.

Passive — This style is based on compliance, and avoiding confrontation at all costs.

Pay attention to what you say and how you say it. Remember, you can't go wrong by treating others with respect.

How long will you hunt for words? Consider, and then we shall speak. (Job 18:2)

Guide us in our daily interactions with others, Prince of Peace.

A Spirit that Soars

After Hurricane Katrina struck New Orleans, Jean Selders returned home expecting a big cleanup and hard work. Instead, with $76 to her name, she encountered complete devastation. "There was nothing left of my house but sludge," she remembers.

She says that she decided to kill herself, but first drove to her church to return clean-up items she had borrowed. A woman at the church looked at Selders and said, "I think you need a hug." Selders says that love saved her.

So she joined other neighbors, offering support and rebuilding homes. "I just kept coming back and helping," she says.

It takes courage and hope to choose life and concern for others amidst devastation. Let love guide your way—no matter what.

Do not let the flood sweep over me, or the deep swallow me up. (Psalm 69:15)

When literal or figurative floods overwhelm us, save us, Divine Lord.

World Changing — Really!

It seems that everywhere you look, there's a book about someone or something that "changed the world."

While it may seem unlikely that the cod fish changed the world, as one text touted, a New York newspaper did unearth a few globe-changing phenomena.

Take, for example, glass. Though its use in decoration and art is ancient, by 1600 or so, window glass, mirrors and lenses were being developed—facilitating extraordinary scientific leaps with telescopes, test tubes, microscopes and the like.

And there was the invention of the compass. Developed around 1300 in Italy, the compass helped navigators to find their way at any time of day or night, resulting in a new world of exploration and commerce.

Seeing or doing things differently can be the breath of fresh air that is, for us, life-changing.

And when you turn to the right or when you turn to the left, your ears shall hear a word behind you, saying, "This is the way; walk in it." (Isaiah 30:21)

When the world's cares wash over me, I look to You, Christ, beloved of my soul.

Fresh Food to the Rescue

Fruit companies dump millions of pounds of still-edible surplus fruits and vegetables each year. Then a non-profit food solicitor in California jumped at the opportunity to rescue this food.

It was generally accepted practice for charities to get donations of extra, sometimes damaged, boxes or cans of food from processors and supermarkets. Then Farm to Family started to gather farm produce—sometimes tons at a time. In its first year, the organization found 10 million pounds of fruits and vegetables to supply food banks around the state.

Now Farm to Family expects to deliver more than 80 million pounds of produce annually. This fresh food will combat both hunger and obesity among poor people.

Never trash what may be another's treasure. Your surplus food and other items are valuable to your poor neighbors.

Give some of your food to the hungry, and some of your clothing to the naked. Give all of your surplus as alms. (Tobit 4:16)

Help us to better use the bounty of Your hand and of Your earth, Generous Creator.

Career Coaching

A career can mean any work from electrician to cardiologist to chef—and far, far more. You can open your children's eyes to the many possibilities from which they can choose.

Read stories to your kids and identify characters' careers. Take your children where they can appreciate other people at work. For example, attend exhibits by artists and photographers; visit zoos, bakeries, fire stations. Tell your children about your own work. If possible, let them see what you do. Find books that encourage career interests.

Evaluate, support and nurture your children's skills and interests. Listen to what others say about them, too. Keep a diary of their activities and accomplishments. Involve your child in school projects and extra-curricular activities that support their skills and interests.

Most importantly, let your children know that you will encourage them in the choices they make.

Amos answered..."I am a herdsman, and a dresser of sycamore trees." (Amos 7:14)

Carpenter from Nazareth, remind us that You blessed work by participating in it.

Thanks! Plain and Simple

Rosie the Riveter, that cultural icon from World War II, represents the American women who worked in factories while men were at war. A West Virginia veterans support group called Thanks! Plain and Simple is recording the stories of local Rosies so they will not be forgotten.

Janice Wright is one who shared her experience with the group. After graduating from high school, she began working at the South Charleston Ordinance Center helping rivet the tails onto Tiny Tim Rockets. Nancy Sipple, another Rosie, tested airplane engine parts for Wright Aeronautical while her husband was in the service. A desire to help their country and the need to support themselves and their families are common themes told by many of the women.

Whether on the job or off, each person can improve this country in some useful way.

I will rejoice in Jerusalem and delight in My people. (Isaiah 65:19)

Remind us to express gratitude to all who serve our community and our nation in vital ways, Lord of all.

From Reading on the Bus

As a school bus driver in Cincinnati, Linda Thieman had time between routes to read books—until the director of religious education at nearby St. Henry's parish noticed.

"She came out one day and said, 'Instead of sitting out here reading a book, would you be interested in teaching a religion class?'" the bus driver recalls.

Thirty years later, Thieman had taught several grade levels, and started a very active youth ministry program. She's even traveled with young people on mission trips around the world, including Haiti, where they met Mother Teresa in the early 1990s.

One former group member, who now heads a similar ministry at another parish, says Thieman's work is "a living legacy that will never end. She has touched the lives of thousands upon thousands of people."

Sometimes what we're called to do is right in front of us. We just need to take a good look around!

**Look at what is before your eyes.
(2 Corinthians 10:7)**

Let me serve You, Father; help me lead others to You.

Family Time

Reggae musician Ziggy Marley is a four-time Grammy winner who advocates peace and love through his music. His latest endeavor, a tribute to his five kids, is a children's album called *Family Time.*

He admits that because he was always busy touring, he was not there for his three oldest as much as he should have been. Learning from past mistakes, he makes an effort to spend time with his younger kids. Furthermore, he has the older ones visit in order to foster relationships among all the children.

Marley believes that "People don't stop playing because they grow old, they grow old because they stop playing." He adds that his children keep him from feeling his age.

Give children the love and attention they need. They will grow up to become loving people.

Jesus...said, "Let the little children come to Me, and do not stop them. (Luke 18:16)

Savior, help parents mirror Your love for their children.

No Longer Lost

Fidele Diing Dhan knew neither God nor a carefree childhood. One of the thousands of so-called "Lost Boys" of Sudan who fled during the long civil war beginning in 1983, Dhan crossed wilderness and desert to escape a land where families were killed, women and girls were raped, and villages were burned.

Dhan, whose story was told in *Maryknoll* magazine, lived in refugee camps for 14 years, before being admitted to the U.S. where he became a citizen and built a new life. Eventually, Dhan worked to bring needed resources, including a medical clinic, back to his land.

The former lost boy found God. And he often shares his favorite scriptural quote, "Knock, and the door will be opened for you."

> **Ask, and it will be given you; search, and you will find; knock, and the door will be opened for you. For everyone who asks receives, and everyone who searches finds, and for everyone who knocks, the door will be opened. (Matthew 7:7-8)**

Thank You, Compassionate Lord, for Your strength.

I'll Do It!

In one recent year, more than 60 million Americans did it.

And, according to one website, there's more of it going on in the state of Utah and in the cities of St. Paul and Minneapolis than anywhere else. Still, from Maine to California, and thousands of places in between, it's a definitive movement: more and more people are volunteering to help their neighbors and community.

"We're seeing a compassion boom," says Nicola Goren of the Corporation for National and Community Service, speaking of the trend toward volunteering. "Because there are so many people struggling now, and so many are neighbors, people are more willing than ever to reach out to others."

Who needs your help today? Take a look around, and lend a hand.

Fulfill the royal law according to the scripture, "You shall love your neighbor as yourself." (James 2:8)

Guide me, Eternal Father, that I may do Your will.

Advancing Kindness

When an embarrassed father told Debbie Mohelnitzky that he could no longer afford to send his son to her daycare center because he lost his job, she told him to bring his son anyway.

Mohelnitzky knew that without daycare, the laid off Wisconsin dad wouldn't be able to look for work. That led to a "pay it forward" campaign. During one week, her center offered out-of-work parents a free half-day of childcare. It didn't even matter if their children were enrolled there; any parent looking for a job was welcome.

All Mohelnitzky asked was that parents agree to do a good deed for someone else within the year. The program was a hit; another daycare center in a nearby town copied the effort.

Our own kind actions can inspire others. As the saying goes, one good deed deserves another.

The measure you give will be the measure you get, and still more will be given you. (Mark 4:24)

Remind us, God, to embody Your kindness and mercy.

Loaves of Love

Karen Kiefer recalls coming home after school to the freshly baked bread her mom made, so she continued the tradition with her own children.

One day, the family made extra loaves for neighbors. The response was so positive, the Kiefers of Wayland, Massachusetts, shared the bread with even more people. "We wrapped the bread and left it on doorsteps with inspirational notes," says Kiefer in *Family Circle* magazine. "It became our way of reaching out."

She and her friend Juliette Fay talked about ways to expand the outreach. Then September 11, 2001 happened. They gave fresh bread and encouraging messages to firefighters and police officers—and urged others to do the same. That's how Spread the Bread was born. Now millions around the USA and the world have participated.

Simple gifts mean so much when offered with love.

(Jesus) took the seven loaves and the fish; and after giving thanks He broke them...and all of them ate and were filled. (Matthew 15:36,37)

Bread of Life, satisfy our hunger for Your Word.

Unique Challenges, Unique Skills

Shortly after the 9/11 terrorist attacks, Dr. Jack Smith of Bayonne, New Jersey, joined the Army Reserve.

As his brother Mark said, Smith always looks for new challenges. "He really wants to be a change agent, where he can make a difference. He's done that."

Captain Smith brought a special set of skills to his post in Afghanistan. A natural athlete, the former police officer had also been a chiropractor, before going on to medical school. Smith's patients in Afghanistan have included a two-year-old girl badly burned in an accident. Although she wasn't wounded in the war, the medical team treated her, earning the gratitude of her father and goodwill in the community.

"Everyone who comes through the door could be my brother, mother or father," said Smith. "That's how they get treated."

Appreciate the unique skills you bring to face the challenges in your life.

Whoever does the will of God is My brother and sister and mother. (Mark 3:35)

May I always seek to see You in my neighbors, Holy God.

Man's Best Friend Just Meowed

Think only dogs are "man's best friend?" Consider Winnie, a domestic shorthair cat of 16 years, who saved the lives of her human owners.

One night in 2007, the Keesling family of Indiana slept soundly, unaware that a crack in the family home's ventilating system was allowing carbon monoxide to pour through the house. As the deadly gas escaped, son Michael fell unconscious, while mom Cathy and husband Eric slowly slipped away.

Winnie, however, began to "pull my hair and yowl in my ear," says Cathy Keesling, who managed to rouse herself out of a stupor and call 911. Thanks to the cat's persistence, the family survived.

Animals are living creatures that can feel comfort as well as pain. Adopt a zero-tolerance stance against animal cruelty and encourage youngsters to have a healthy respect for God's creatures.

> **When the bow is in the clouds, I will see it and remember the everlasting covenant between God and every living creature of all flesh that is on earth. (Genesis 9:16)**

Guide us in protecting the helpless, Mighty God.

Learning Curve

Do you know when the Civil War was fought?

Probably not, if you're an American teenager. At least that's what a survey commissioned by Common Core, a research and advocacy organization, indicates. That study revealed that a significant proportion of teenagers live in "stunning ignorance" of history and literature.

Common Core is pressing for more liberal arts in public schools. The group finds the current curriculum too focused on test scores for reading and mathematics. In fact, the Center on Education Policy in Washington, D.C. estimated that more than 60 percent of U.S. school systems had added an average of three hours of math or reading instruction a week at the expense of time for other subjects.

No matter our age, each of us remains a student of the world around us. Look for the lesson in every moment.

Teach...knowledge and prudence to the young. (Proverbs 1:4)

Lord of truth and knowledge, I am listening; teach me Your ways.

Minding My Business

Americans are making it clear that they want to own their own businesses. A recent Gallup poll revealed that more than 60 per cent of people want to be their own bosses. And they're doing just that in increasing numbers.

"We're in the midst of a boom in home-based businesses, and it shows no sign of slowing," says economist Paul Zane Pilzer.

Many factors have fueled the trend in recent years, including people wanting to better control how they spend their time; corporations cutting some previously guaranteed benefits like health care and pensions; and a shaky economy that meant the lay-off of vast numbers of workers.

No matter who owns or runs a business, every person's work should always reflect the best of their talent and effort.

**The people had a mind to work.
(Nehemiah 4:6)**

I offer You my labor this day, my Master; bless the work of my hands.

Dwindling Attendance, Persistent Memories

The Hancock Village School in Hancock, Vermont, first opened in 1801, when Thomas Jefferson was president of the United States.

More than 200 years later, it shut its doors. Because of fewer students in attendance and rising costs, the majority of voters in the town elected to close the elementary school. Still, residents lamented the closing. "When you've lost the heart of your town, you've lost a history that is pretty hard to match," says the school's now-former principal.

What institutions and businesses in your community serve as its heart? What can you do to have them recognized and preserved?

He has made everything suitable for its time; moreover He has put a sense of past and future into (peoples') minds. (Ecclesiastes 3:11)

Help me adhere to traditions that bring us closer, Abba, and that serve the good of all.

Making Connections

Some churches in the U.S. link with sister parishes in other parts of the world, providing a rewarding experience for all.

In what is becoming an annual tradition, a group from a tri-parish community in St. Cloud Diocese, Minnesota, travels to a Mexican village in the foothills of the Sierra Madre de Chiapas mountains to help construct schools and houses.

"I do not speak Spanish," said Gary Meyer, one of the Minnesotans, "and our Mexican project coordinator could not speak a word of English." Yet their construction work proceeded.

Some women found common ground in their cooking, baking and preparations for special occasions such as a "quinceanera" party honoring a girl's 15th birthday. And when the youngsters weren't lending a hand, they organized soccer and volleyball games.

Connect with people from other cultures and backgrounds and discover how much you have in common.

Declare His glory among the nations, His marvelous works among all the people. (1 Chronicles 16:24)

Thank you, Holy God, for all Your nations. Help us complement each other's strengths and weaknesses.

We're More Than Stereotypes

In reporting for the *New York Times*, Tamar Lewis described a National Science Foundation study which shows that girls do as well as boys on standardized math tests. This appears to contradict a persistent and commonly held belief that math is too tough for girls.

"The stereotype that boys do better at math is still widely held by teachers and parents," said Dr. Janet Hyde, a professor at the University of Wisconsin who led the study. They guide girls, giving them advice about what courses to take, what careers to pursue. "I still hear anecdotes about guidance counselors steering girls away from engineering, telling them they won't be able to do the math," says Hyde.

The major challenges of our time are too complex to dampen the hopes of students, girls or boys. It's time to allow all young people to fulfill their potential.

Do not provoke your children to anger, but bring them up in the discipline and instruction of the Lord. (Ephesians 6:4)

Paraclete, inspire us to use well the talents You gave us.

Living With Integrity

In tough economic times, how tempting would it be to keep $500 in cash that you found?

Amy Cotter of Bedford, New York, had just finished loading groceries into her car and pushing the empty cart back to the store. But as she prepared to drive away, she realized her purse was still in the shopping cart.

"By the time I got back to the cart my purse was gone. I was upset especially because I had just cashed a $500 check."

Cotter never thought she'd see her handbag again. However, within half an hour she got a call from the woman who had found it. "She saw the cash in my wallet and thought it would be safest to return it personally."

Doing the right thing isn't always easy, but it is best—for our own souls as well as other people.

So my honesty will answer for me later. (Genesis 30:33)

May honesty and integrity flourish in my heart, Holy Redeemer.

Teaching Values

Learning is stifled in an atmosphere of harassment or fear of violence. No place is appropriate for such behavior, especially not a classroom of vulnerable youngsters.

With this in mind, Peter Yarrow and others work to end bullying and encourage respect in schools. Long devoted to social causes as a member of the renowned folk group Peter, Paul and Mary, Yarrow founded Operation Respect to promote character education.

The nonprofit organization distributes resources to fulfill its mission to "assure each child and youth a respectful, safe and compassionate climate of learning where their academic, social and emotional development can take place free of bullying, ridicule and violence."

The program uses music, video, conflict resolution training and other tools to assist educators in reaching students.

Not only teachers and parents, but children, too, can be enlisted in the effort to reduce cruelty.

Violence shall no more be heard in your land... you shall call your walls Salvation and your gates Praise. (Isaiah 60:18)

Loving Father, remove all meanness and malice from my mind and heart.

Second Helpings, Second Chances

Most of us know the effort and planning that can go into the preparation of a single family meal. Imagine preparing and delivering 2,900 meals, each week! That's what Second Helpings does.

It's a 10-year old Indianapolis agency that offers free, nutritious meals and second chances to low-income people. Second Helpings not only uses rescued food—unused food from local restaurants—to serve nearly all these meals to the needy, it also works to eliminate hunger in the area in other ways.

For instance, the group conducts cooking classes to train unemployed or underemployed adults for careers in the restaurant industry, thereby providing further support to low-income adults.

All of us, at one time or another, could use a "second chance." How can you give a fresh start to those enduring hard times?

Stretch out your hand to the poor. (Sirach 7:32)

How can I extend my superabundant blessings to those who lack even the basics of a human life, Generous Giver?

From Dropout to Scholar

Jamar Whaley scored high on intelligence tests in high school—but dropped out before graduation.

After working for a time, Whaley earned his high school equivalency degree, and then applied and was admitted to Queens College in New York City. He even got a scholarship, awarded only to the top 10 students seeking admission.

"My great-grandmother always thought there was a chance for me," Whaley says of the woman who raised him since infancy. "Now I want to help out and do for the world what my great-grandmother has done for me. I want to make sure others can have a life and excel after they have underachieved."

Whaley has already won several awards for young scientists and has conducted research at Yale University.

Who in our lives needs a helping hand? Today may be your day to make a difference!

Give victory with Your right hand, and answer me, so that those whom you love may be rescued. (Psalm 108:6)

In all the moments of my life, I draw strength from You, Father of my being.

The Family That Reads Together

According to one study, the number of kids who are read to every day drops significantly at age nine. But some experts suggest that raising a confident, lifelong reader requires that you keep reading—together, as a family.

In fact, reading aloud can expand your child's vocabulary, and your conversations can help young people understand and enjoy more. Here are some ways to facilitate your "read-together" ritual:

- **Pick age-appropriate books.** The goal of the experience is understanding and enjoyment.
- **Listen to audiobooks.** Press "play" during car rides or after dinner.
- **Revisit favorites.** Discussions can focus on subtleties and move beyond just the plot.

Family time—no matter what you do—is sacred, nurturing experiences of love and acceptance.

They stood up in their place and read from the book of the law of the Lord their God. (Nehemiah 9:3)

We are Your children, Lord God. We give You thanks and praise for all You are, for all Your generosity.

You Choose the News

Stories about the horror of war around the globe often appear next to headlines such as "Bacon Flavored Jelly Beans!"

That's what you'll find on Digg.com, a website created by Kevin Rose, who's been obsessed with computers since childhood. Inspired by social networking sites that allowed users to post photographs and videos, and then talk about them, Rose decided to start a website that took that approach to news. Users post stories and images found on the websites of large newspapers and smaller blog sites, and then decide whether they "digg" or like the items, or "bury" them because they don't.

Launched in November 2004, Digg is today among the most-visited websites in the United States.

No matter the day, we should rejoice in the greatest news of all—God loves us! Now that's a headline you can "digg"!

For God so loved the world that He gave His only Son, so that everyone who believes in Him may...have eternal life. (John 3:16)

I seek Your wisdom, Master; show me Your way.

Herding Sheep — Yesterday and Today

For centuries, shepherds throughout Europe would annually move their flocks from the mountains to lower, warmer areas each autumn. By the 1950s the sheep were generally put on flatbed trucks, instead.

But a few years ago, Tracturo 3000 was begun by local activists in Italy to celebrate the tradition by walking the sheep from L'Aquila in the Apennine Mountains of Abruzzo more than 150 miles southeast to Foggia in the Puglia area.

Tracturo 3000 aims to re-chart the original trails and get them recognized by UNESCO as heritage of humanity sites. It also encourages tourists to walk the trails, eat and stay at inns and taverns; visit towns and villages along the way to shop and enjoy the artistic heritage and natural beauty of the area.

Consider the past as well as the present and future when you look around this world of ours.

The Lord is my shepherd — He makes me lie down in green pastures; He leads me beside still waters. (Psalm 23:1,2)

Guide and guard all people struggling to recover from natural disasters and other crises, Good Shepherd.

Easy For Us, Not Machines

People have the ability to recognize faces and, it turns out, so do honeybees. Computers don't, at least not yet.

Bees seem to employ the same method as humans, known as configured processing, according to *The Journal of Experimental Biology*.

As computer scientists and technologists learn more about facial recognition, they may one day develop sophisticated machines able to identify the same person despite changes. Such machines might learn to recognize the same people after their hair has grown, when they have sunglasses on, or after they have aged. These are tasks humans can perform but which computers struggle to replicate. One practical application might be in airport security.

As useful as it may be, many people probably still take comfort in knowing that machines can't yet do everything that people—and honeybees—can do.

The Lord make His face to shine upon you, and be gracious to you. (Numbers 6:25)

Help me to see Your holy face in each person I meet, Jesus, my Lord, my life.

The Power of the Family Dinner

Times are hard, and people are busy. Few of us have the luxury of enjoying a full, sit-down meal every night of the week, surrounded by loved ones and relaxed conversation.

Yet, research has illustrated the critically important role the family dinner plays in a child's development. Study after study shows that kids who dine with their families on a regular basis are healthier, less likely to be overweight, and less likely to smoke, drink or use drugs.

In addition, kids who are treated to a family dinner are also more likely to do well in school and just plain feel happier. Dining with parents offers kids yet another benefit: Kids learn conversational skills, manners and values. Even if you can't do it every day, dine as a family as often as possible.

Perhaps the most important thing parents can "serve up" to their kids at dinnertime is their presence and attention.

Believe in the Lord Jesus, and you will be saved, you and your household. (Acts 16:31)

God, bless all who raise children in these uncertain times.

When Sleep is the Rx

This wondrous human body of ours has an amazing way of self-regulating, especially when we are sleep-deprived. In fact, our bodies let us know when we are not getting enough sleep. Sadly, so many of us are so used to going without sufficient sleep, we hardly notice the signs.

For example, if you find yourself overwhelmed by even simple decisions, a sleep deficit could be the cause. When we are tired, we are less able to distinguish between important and non-essential information, which is part of decision-making.

Another sign is constant hunger. If you are eating all day long, but still feel hungry, sleep deprivation could be the culprit. Chronic sleep loss disrupts blood-sugar levels and causes the body to feel continuously hungry, mainly because of stress.

Finally, if you suffer from one cold after another, get more sleep. Fighting infection is easier for a well-rested body.

Take care of yourself. Your body is your responsibility.

When you lie down, your sleep will be sweet. (Proverbs 3:24)

Help me develop healthful living habits, Heavenly Father.

Love's Price

During World War II, Irena Sendler, a senior social worker, got a pass to visit the Warsaw Ghetto daily during a typhoid outbreak. She helped bring 450,000 sick, starving and dying Jews food, medicines and clothing.

She also got false documents for 2500 Jewish infants and children whom they smuggled out and sent to religious institutions and families. Sendler noted the children's original and new names in code before her arrest in 1943, hoping that some would be reunited with their families. Sadly, most were not.

Crippled for the rest of her life by torture, she never betrayed those Jewish children. Israel's Yad Vashem gave her the Righteous Among the Nations title in 1965. She was made an honorary Israeli in 1991 and in 2003 she was honored by Poland.

"The world can be better, if there's love, tolerance, and humility," Sendler said.

Show love, tolerance and humility today.

From (the Israelites), according to the flesh, comes the Messiah...God blessed forever. (Romans 9:5)

Reward those who oppose anti-Semitism, God.

From a Farm to the Hungry

Pachamama Farm produced 25,713 pounds of fruits and vegetables in one year. At $1.40 per pound, the value of organic produce in New York, the farm could earn $36,000 annually. Pachamama, however, belongs to the Maryknoll Fathers and Brothers and feeds hungry people in Westchester County for free.

Maryknoll affiliate Mary J. Murphy developed the idea of the farm which was originally designed to reward shareholders with produce in exchange for their support. Realizing that giving away the produce would create less paperwork and benefit more people, Murphy and her associates at Pachamama now distribute food to the poor at no cost through seven food pantries.

No one needs to be hungry. Share the bounty of God's earth with others.

I was hungry and you gave Me food, I was thirsty and you gave Me...drink.
(Matthew 25:35)

How can we help satisfy the hunger and thirst of the poor, Loving Lord?

A Game that Ended (and Started) It All

Back in October, 1969, a college football game took place in Tampa Stadium that forever changed the way the sport was played on a collegiate level.

Both coaches—a white man and a black man—had decided that the days of single-race football games in the South were over. No more blacks only playing blacks or whites playing whites. Jake Gaither of Florida A & M and Fran Curci of the University of Tampa shook hands before the game started.

"Jake, this is bigger than I thought it would be," said Curci.

"Not me," said Gaither.

They watched as their teams played in a city that had suffered a violent race riot just two years earlier. The event, which came off without a hitch, showed that an area once so deeply divided could change and heal.

Do what you can to ensure justice and equality for all.

Thus says the Lord: Maintain justice, and do what is right. (Isaiah 56:1)

Eradicate prejudice from our hearts, Prince of Peace.

Healing, Hope and a Better Future

When Theresa Karminski Burke began her career as a counselor, she noticed that a number of her clients' mental health issues were rooted in abortions they had had. So she decided to find a way to help them.

In 1986, Burke founded Rachel's Vineyard, a therapeutic support group for women who have had abortions. Today 90 teams in 45 states and 17 foreign countries help women of various faiths deal with their pain. In addition, the staff and volunteers have expanded their efforts to help victims of sexual abuse through their new Grief to Grace program.

"Real healing transforms and makes you better than you used to be," says Burke.

It's hard to deal with pain from a difficult past, but keep hope in your heart and the future will reveal God's peace.

We have hope in God that He will soon have mercy on us. (2 Maccabees 2:18)

Bless my body and soul with Your grace-filled mercy, Loving Lord.

Eighth-Graders Steal the Show

More than 400 charitable donors shared conversation and steaks at the annual Inner-City Scholarship Fund award dinner, where the generosity of hundreds helped raise almost $1.6 million.

The fund supports more than 38,000 students in over 100 Archdiocesan schools in New York City. The fund's Emergency Tuition Assistance account helps families who face unexpected crises, but who desperately want their children to remain enrolled in Catholic school.

While many donated impressive amounts, the donation that garnered a standing ovation was that of the eighth-grade students of Resurrection School in Rye, New York. The students held a car wash and raised $1,000 for the Fund, which they presented personally to Archbishop Timothy Dolan.

Young people have a tremendous capacity for compassion, love and forgiveness. Treat children with respect and kindness.

I was overjoyed to find some of your children walking in the truth. (2 John 4)

Protect Your little ones, Eternal Father, and help us to imitate You.

Doing Your Part with Francis

Francis of Assisi is one of the best known and widely honored saints. But why has he attracted such attention over the last 800 years? Here's one possible answer:

"What must be understood about Francis is the centrality of the Word of God in his life," wrote Rev. Roch Niemier, OFM, author of *In the Footsteps of Francis and Clare.* "The Word became flesh, Incarnate. This is the defining hallmark of the Franciscan gift to Christian spirituality. God became one of us. Francis' preaching was effective because he lived the Word. He embodied the Word. When he proclaimed the Word, people saw the Word come to life."

As Francis of Assisi lay dying, he said, "I have done my part. May Christ teach you to do yours."

May that be true for each of us.

(Jesus) said...'love the Lord your God with all your heart, and with all your soul, and with all your mind...love your neighbor as yourself.' (Matthew 22:37,39)

Holy Spirit, guide me in walking with Jesus—the path which so many good, holy people have walked in faith.

Reclaim the Streets

Cars dominate the urban landscape. Policy and planning accommodates their use, which further adds to their permanence in urban settings. Mark Gorton, however, believes that cities should serve people rather than cars.

Gorton is the founder and executive director of The Open Planning Project, an organization that questions the role of cars, especially in cities. It will take years to decrease the dependency on cars, but Gorton lauds current efforts to reclaim the streets. For example, cars have been banned near Times Square and Herald Square in Manhattan. Without cars, these areas are more open to the public. Gorton's group is also educating youngsters on transportation alternatives.

Lessen your reliance on cars. Walk more. Appreciate your surroundings: urban, suburban or rural.

The people of Nineveh saw (Tobit) walking along in full vigor and with no one leading him...(God) had restored his sight. (Tobit 11:16,17)

Get us up on our feet and out the door into Your lovely world, Creator.

Teens Making a Difference

Two years ago, eight 14-year-old girls from Long Island, New York, watched a news report about child trafficking in Ghana. They were horrified to learn that for as little as $20 many Ghanaian families unknowingly sell their children into lives of servitude.

Seeing this as an opportunity to help others, they agreed to save at least one child, but "once we started, we couldn't stop," explains Ariel Stern, one of the group. They began a charity called One is Greater Than None (1>0). Designing and selling jewelry and T-shirts, the group raises money for the International Organization for Migration, which rescues children. To date, these dedicated friends have saved 48 Ghanaian children.

No matter where you're from or what your age, you will always have the power to make a positive difference in others' lives.

Do good; seek justice, rescue the oppressed. (Isaiah 1:17)

Inspire teens to whole-hearted action on behalf of those in need at home and abroad, Spirit of Joy.

"Busting" Health Myths

Recent scientific studies have shed new light on common health myths.

- Drink eight glasses of water every day? That's about the 2.5 liters adults were told to drink in 1945. Most of this water comes from the food you eat, so there is no need to drink so much.

- Do people warn you about getting sick in cold weather? Colds and flu come from viruses, not the weather, though some viruses are more common during winter because you are indoors more.

- Think drinking more orange juice will prevent illness? Vitamin C will neither protect you from illness, nor ease your symptoms if you are sick.

Learn the facts so that you will be better equipped to care for the marvelous body and mind God has given you.

Before you fall ill, take care of your health. (Sirach 18:19)

Divine Creator, help me distinguish fact from fiction.

Fighting to Remember

Sent to a labor camp in Poland after his family's flour mill was seized by Nazis, Miles Lerman managed to escape. He spent the rest of World War II working with others to thwart the Germans.

After the war, he married and traveled to America, where he eventually built two successful businesses. But Lerman's burning desire was that no one would forget the horrors of the Holocaust. He helped raise millions for the Holocaust Memorial Museum in Washington, D.C., and was its founding chair. He established the museum's Committee on Conscience to raise awareness of genocide today, in places like Darfur. He even returned to his native Poland to help build an appropriate memorial for those who had died in the concentration camps.

Lerman was 88 when he died—his legacy a lesson on working for good, in spite of the evil around you.

Do not be overcome by evil, but overcome evil with good. (Romans 12:21)

My trust and my hope rest in You, compassionate Lord.

The Art of Sports

Today, sports news seems focused on who drafted whom, steroid use and scandals of various types. But there's more to athletics than this.

Sports writer Dave Zirin writes his *Edge of Sports* column with a refreshing voice, looking at what happens on the field as a sociological statement. For example, in a piece about game violence, Zirin wrote, "Beneath the veneer, college football is a multibillion-dollar spectacle of unpaid labor and unhinged fandom." More than that, he sees sports as not just a game, "It's physical expression, it's beauty, and it's been the site of some of the most electric struggles of the century."

Athletics is indeed a unique human expression. Concentrate on its positive aspects and encourage others to do the same.

Run with perseverance. (Hebrews 12:1)

Help athletes avoid all that detracts from sportsmanship, Just God, and guide them in seeking all that's healthy for body and soul.

Sequoyah's Legacy

The man named Sequoyah, also known as George Gist, was born in 1770 in Tennessee. His father was from England; his mother was from a distinguished Cherokee family. After watching white settlers communicate by making marks on paper, he was inspired to create a Cherokee writing system for his people.

Despite the criticism of friends who thought he was being absurd, Sequoyah started to devise his system in 1809. Ten years later, he had completed a script of 85 characters, each of which represented a sound in the Cherokee language. Within a few years, most Cherokees had adopted Sequoyah's method, the only known instance of an individual developing an entirely new writing system.

Find the strength within yourself to achieve your goals. Don't let others' negative attitudes hinder you.

Happy are those who persevere. (Daniel 12:12)

Blessed Trinity, grant me Your gift of determination.

An Educational Effort

South Central Los Angeles school bus driver Tanya Walters so loves traveling that she formed the GodParents Youth Organization (GYO).

GYO brings high school students across the country to historical sites. Students with below average grades can apply, but they are accepted only if they raise their grades in ninety days.

Students have traveled to such places as the Grand Canyon, Chicago, Niagara Falls, and New Orleans. One of the first students to participate, Takeisha McComb, says touring the country was "a purpose-driven life." After each visit, Walters would assign the students homework and quizzes. One student says she "rode them hard to make them learn."

Walters believes the program is a way of recovering teens' "idealism, energy and creativity." She wants "them to dream and believe they can do anything."

You too can dream. Explore all the possibilities.

Love your neighbor as yourself.
(Galatians 5:14)

How can we help teens believe in themselves, Jesus?

Changing Images

The memory haunted Army Sergeant Gunnar Swanson—the image of his pointing an M-16 rifle at a young Iraqi boy, warning him not to come closer. The boy froze, then quickly fled.

Swanson and his fellow soldiers had first enjoyed good relationships with Iraq's youth, but then many young people were forced to join insurgent groups, making them a threat. And yet, for Swanson, pointing a gun at the child was an extreme measure.

Unable to shake the experience, Swanson decided to do something positive to replace the image flashing in his mind. After leaving the army, he moved from his Florida home to Minnesota to work for War Kids Relief, an organization that aids children in Iraq and Afghanistan and educates American youngsters about their peers. Today, Swanson sees images of now hope-filled youth.

Troubling events affect us, but it's never too late to choose a new direction.

For the Lord will be your confidence and will keep your foot from being caught.
(Proverbs 3:26)

May I see You always, Lord, in all I meet this day.

Changing Careers the Smart Way

With people now living longer than ever, it's not uncommon for some people to have two, even three careers in a lifetime. Changing careers can be made easier with a few innovative tactics, says career coach Pamela Skillings.

Volunteer. It can be an ideal way to "try out" a new career while giving back to your community, or contributing to a cause in which you believe. In addition, volunteering can also translate into a terrific skill-building opportunity.

Take a class. Peruse the course catalog of your local community college, where classes are often reasonably priced and easily accessible.

Make money from a hobby. Ease into a new field by marketing your product or service on a small scale.

Discover and cultivate as many skills and interests as possible.

It is God's gift that all should...take pleasure in all their toil. (Ecclesiastes 3:13)

Help me find joy in all my labors, Messiah.

Repaving Wall Street

Christine Ward is a philanthropist who worked to bring relief to victims of the 2004 tsunami in Asia and the 2005 earthquake in Pakistan. She is now focusing her efforts on bringing aid to Darfur, where 300,000 people have been killed and more than 2 million displaced.

Ward's charity, the Darfur Project, reaches out to large, powerful American financial companies to fund the purchase and transportation of supplies to Darfur. Ward feels that she is giving corporations the opportunity to do something positive with their wealth for some of the world's neediest people.

There is suffering everywhere. It's within your power to help change that situation by assisting one person at a time.

Has not God chosen the poor in the world to be rich in faith and to be heirs of the kingdom? (James 2:5)

Inspire businesspeople to put human need before the desire for profits, Holy Wisdom.

Play it Safe; Reduce Your Risk

It's a sobering statistic—one in eight women in the U.S. will develop breast cancer at some point in her life.

Take heart, though: Eighty-eight percent of them survive at least 10 years after their diagnosis. Even more encouraging is the fact that women can reduce their risk of breast cancer while improving their overall health. Follow these steps:

- **Exercise.** Walking just two and a half hours per week can cut breast cancer risk by nearly 20 percent. In addition, walking helps boost energy and the immune system.

- **Limit alcohol intake.** Even moderate alcohol consumption raises breast cancer risk.

- **Get screening mammograms.** According to the American Cancer Society, the five-year survival rate for women who catch breast cancer at the earliest stage is 98 percent.

All women and men have an obligation to care for their own well-being and that of their families.

Take care of your health. (Sirach 18:19)

Remind me, Lord, of my duty to care for myself.

John Brown — Hero or Terrorist?

John Brown launched a bloody attack on Harper's Ferry, West Virginia, in 1859. His attempt to end slavery left some 15 dead including a free black man. Brown himself was tried for treason, convicted and executed.

Historians' judgement of Brown remains split: some credit him with forcing tension over slavery into a final resolution; others condemn his actions.

In fact, in 1959, as America planned to mark the centennial of the Civil War, officials largely left Brown out of the discussion. Fifty years later, some even label Brown and his followers terrorists. "They firmly believe what they're doing is right," said Gerry Gaumer, a spokesman for the Park Service in Washington, D.C. "But is there a better way?"

Our choices should reflect our standards and beliefs, but should always consider the consequences to those around us.

Thus says the Lord...ask for the ancient paths, where the good way lies; and walk in it, and find rest for your souls. (Jeremiah 6:16)

Help me choose the right path, Your path, Savior.

Charitable Works the Creative Way

Matt Knapp used to spend his own money on supplies for his middle-school students. Now, he relies on Extras for Creative Learning, a non-profit group that funnels office supplies and other business surplus to teachers, daycare providers and parents.

Members pay a small annual fee for eight visits to the group's warehouse, where they can take as many supplies as they need. Knapp usually stocks up on poster boards, drawing paper, markers, pens, binders and sometimes craft materials.

Jodi Schmidt, the organization's director, says that the center receives items that businesses would otherwise throw away. Now, because of the center's creative approach to charitable works, donating businesses can enjoy a tax credit instead.

A little creativity goes a long way. How can you connect someone's generosity to a person in need?

It is a question of fair balance between your present abundance and their need.
(2 Corinthians 8:13-14)

Inspire businesses and individuals to share from their surplus, Holy Spirit.

Is Coffee Good For You?

Coffee, or more specifically, caffeine, can have desirable effects—within limits.

Weight Watchers Magazine quotes Lawrence L. Spriet, a professor of health and nutritional science, who says, "Caffeine has a powerful effect on the brain. It increases alertness, makes exercise feel easier, and counteracts your brain's response to pain."

Caffeine can't help you lose weight by increasing metabolism, but it won't dehydrate you as previously thought. Consuming a moderate amount of caffeine doesn't appear to create heart problems. However, those with hypertension should check with their doctors. Also, watch the sugar content of caffeinated energy drinks, particularly if you're watching your weight.

As with any health concerns, it pays to do your own research to see what's right for you.

Moderation is usually a key to a healthy life of body, mind and soul.

Keep sound wisdom and prudence, and they will be life for your soul and adornment for your neck. (Proverbs 3:22)

Almighty God, guide my choices in all things.

What Makes You Truly Happy?

Cars, computers, condos, clothing! New possessions make many of us happy, at least for a little while.

Of course certain possessions become keepsakes and develop sentimental value. But studies suggest that in the long run we're more satisfied with experiences, for example, attending ballgames or concerts, than with most material objects.

"The initial joy of acquiring a new object fades over time as people become accustomed to seeing it every day," according to Elizabeth Landau quoting various experts. "Experiences on the other hand, continue to provide happiness through memories long after the event occurred."

Writing for CNN.com, Landau cites Cornell University psychology professor Thomas Gilovich who says experiences form "powerful and important memories that I wouldn't trade for anything in the world."

We might all benefit from reflecting on those things in life that have made us the happiest.

Happy are you, O Israel! Who is like you, a people saved by the Lord! (Deuteronomy 33:29)

Thank You, gracious Father, for the joy You share with us!

Healing House

When her nephew was hospitalized in another state, Mary Keough watched her sister and brother-in-law struggle to find a place to stay during his treatment. So when a building became available in her Syracuse neighborhood, she knew what to do.

Keough started Sarah House in 1994 for the families of those receiving medical treatment nearby. Named for Sarah, the wife of the Old Testament patriarch Abraham, Sarah House provides guests—more than 7,000 since it opened—a sympathetic shoulder to lean on as well as a place to stay.

In the midst of life's difficulties, there's comfort to be found both in offering others compassion and in receiving their compassion.

The compassion of human beings is for their neighbors, but the compassion of the Lord is for every living thing. (Sirach 18:13)

Help us accept and give compassion, Merciful Savior.

Overcoming Obstacles

It would never be easy for the Bangladeshi youth. Writing in *Maryknoll Magazine*, Father Douglas Venne, M.M., tells the story of Bimol Marandi, who lost his arms at age seven after handling a live electric wire.

The road from childhood to young adulthood was rocky, but ultimately made smoother by the Taizé Brothers, a Christian community founded in France in 1940 during the Nazi terror. Today their ministry includes helping physically and mentally challenged people to overcome obstacles.

Once in the Taizé community, Marandi learned to manage daily living skills independently. He also discovered a keen artistic ability which he worked hard to cultivate, learning to paint with his feet and his mouth.

We can overcome much with the help of others.

You do well if you really fulfill the royal law according to the scripture, "You shall love your neighbor as yourself." (James 2:8)

Bless my body, my mind, my soul, Creator, and help me use my whole being to serve You.

Attitude Adjustments

A person's attitude is not set; it's a choice, says John C. Maxwell, author of *The Difference Maker: Making Your Attitude Your Greatest Asset.*

He believes that the way we think determines our attitudes, and that a daily evaluation of one's thinking and overall attitude is in order.

"If you take responsibility for your attitude—recognizing that it can change how you live, managing it every day, and cultivating and developing positive thoughts and habits," Maxwell says, "then you can make your attitude your greatest asset.

"It can become the difference maker in your life, opening doors and helping you overcome great obstacles," he concludes.

So, every day, in every way, think—and you'll be—positive!

God chose to make known...the glory of this mystery, which is Christ in you, the hope of glory. (Colossians 2:27)

Fill me with hope, Lord, that I may live joyfully.

A Simple Start is All it Takes

Did you know that studies show that nearly half of all people who volunteer started because they were asked to do so by someone else?

According to *USA Weekend Magazine*, which hosts an annual Make a Difference Day, simply enlisting the help of even one person could lead to a lifetime of service.

Take Lisa Buksbaum, founder of Soaringwords, a support network for chronically ill children. Last year, she coordinated more than 100 volunteers at various locations throughout North America to create handmade gifts with inspirational messages for hospitalized children.

Then there's Luke Metropulos, a teen who gives the fish he catches off the Florida coast to a food pantry. Now he is teaching disadvantaged children how to fish and, along with other volunteers, taking a group of these youngsters on a fishing trip.

One person can make a difference. Become that person!

It is He who remembered us in our low estate... who gives food to all flesh, for His steadfast love endures forever. (Psalm 136:23, 25)

Remind me, Blessed Trinity, that with Your grace all things are possible.

One Logo, Broad Recognition

Sometimes, fame and recognition spring from unlikely events. Take Donal McLaughlin, Jr. who said that he "dreamed once of seeing my designs in brick and stone."

The son of an architect, this Yale graduate began his career as an industrial designer, finding recognition as a designer for major events, such as the 1939 World's Fair. He also had large corporate clients such as Tiffany & Co. for whom he designed the interior of its flagship Manhattan store.

Yet, it was a small badge that earned McLaughlin his most memorable honor. In 1945, he designed "a round emblem showing latitude and longitude lines" over the continents, then added olive branches, a symbol for peace. This image was ultimately chosen as the official logo of the United Nations. Today, it's recognized around the world.

If you spread them far enough, your talents might take you places you never dreamed possible.

**I have given skill to all the skillful.
(Exodus 31:6)**

Stir our creativity to life, Paraclete.

Shakespeare and Faith

When writer Joseph Pearce reads William Shakespeare's plays such as *Hamlet* and *King Lear*, he sees evidence that Shakespeare was Catholic.

Pearce has penned two books on the world-famous English writer. The first examined Shakespeare's possible Catholicism, as gleaned from the details of his life. The most recent offering looks at the proof of his faith as found in the text of his plays.

"Since the evidence shows that Shakespeare was a believing Catholic, it is clear that seeing his play through his Catholic eyes is the best way of understanding the deepest meanings that they convey," Pearce concludes.

How is your faith reflected in your words and actions? Take time out and look at yourself.

The people who are loyal to their God shall stand firm and take action. (Daniel 11:32)

Master, grant that I may act always with a loving heart.

Healthy Habits

Pre-diabetes as well as type-2 diabetes are on the rise in the U.S., writes Michele Bender in *Weight Watchers Magazine*. This trend is a serious danger to health, but there are lifestyle changes that can make a positive difference in reducing your risk of diabetes and improving your overall health:

- Lose excess weight.
- Get regular exercise.
- Manage stress.
- Brush and floss. Researchers found that people with periodontal disease were twice as likely to develop type 2 diabetes.
- Eat high-fiber foods, including whole grains, fruits and vegetables.
- Get enough sleep.

Ask your doctor to evaluate your risks and help you do what's necessary for your well-being.

I will restore health to you, and your wounds I will heal, says the Lord. (Jeremiah 30:17)

It's hard to change my habits, gracious Creator, but help me to care for my health and that of my loved ones.

The Violin Families

Carleen Hutchins didn't just make violins. She re-imagined what they could be.

Her hands-on acoustic research led her to create a family of eight instruments proportional in size and pitch, and known collectively as the new violin family or the violin octet. Hutchins made eight such violin families during her 98-year lifetime. Composers Henry Brant and Frank Lewin wrote pieces specifically for the octet. In fact, it was at the request of Brant that Hutchins began work on the violin family.

Born in Springfield, Massachusetts, Hutchins started out as a high school science teacher. She had made conventional violins before the octet. Renowned cellist Yo-Yo Ma even recorded a classical piece using one of Hutchins' alto violins.

The work of our hands gives praise to the Creator who endowed us with unique gifts—and is a gift to the world around us.

Since you are eager for spiritual gifts, strive to excel in them for building up the church.
(1 Corinthians 14:12)

We will sing Your praises, Lord of time and eternity, in thanksgiving for all You have given us.

Sharing Rides and Good Ideas

Would you welcome a good idea meant to reduce your stress levels? Of course. And even more so if it also eases smog and traffic congestion.

Commuter Connections, an established ride-sharing agency in the metro Washington area, recently expanded beyond its usual clientele of daily carpoolers to include people during leisure time.

"If you're waiting to get into an event, wondering if you're going to be on time to see the kickoff or the beginning of the concert, that's stressful," said Nick Ramos, director of Commuter Connections. "You want to go and have a good time, not get stuck in traffic."

It's useful to have options when mass transit isn't practical. Try connecting with neighbors so you can use one car instead of several. And if you have other good ideas, pass them along to the folks around you.

O Lord...make successful the way I am going. (Genesis 24:42)

Grant me the grace to use my creativity well, Paraclete.

First Welcomed by a Camel

A 200-mile journey on rocky roads in brutal heat…a man in a turban, seated on a camel, blowing an eight-foot-long trumpet of welcome … that's what greeted Father Peter Otillio, a Dominican missionary from New Orleans, on his arrival in Nigeria in 1959.

When another priest that day referred to that place as his home, Father Otillio thought, "Who could ever call this God-forsaken place home?"

Five decades later, this Catholic priest is still in Nigeria—and very much at home serving his neighbors. "All we do is the Lord's," he says, "and when you place the task in His hands, it soon becomes one that is even joyful."

Facing the unfamiliar may make us want to retreat. But in forging ahead, we may find great delight, even hope.

Rejoice in hope, be patient in suffering, persevere in prayer. (Romans 12:12)

Walk with me, Father of all people, that I may follow the right path, Your path.

Doctor in Charge

"Through floods and fires and severe want, Regina Benjamin has refused to give up." That's the description offered of Dr. Regina Benjamin when she was appointed the Surgeon General for the United States in 2009.

Her perseverance has paid off for herself and others. Growing up poor in Alabama, she repaid government aid for her medical studies by building a clinic in a small town outside of Mobile. When Hurricane Georges sent five feet of water surging into that clinic in 1998, Dr. Benjamin made house calls until it was rebuilt. When Hurricane Katrina destroyed the clinic seven years later, she mortgaged her own home to rebuild it. In the meantime, she traveled by jeep to find and care for her patients.

All around us are examples of those who sacrifice and serve; take note and say, "Thank you!"

Many will give thanks on our behalf for the blessing granted us through the prayers of the many. (2 Corinthians 1:11)

Heal me, Lord; send Your compassion my way and help me share it with others.

In Praise of Pumpkins

It's the perfect vegetable for those watching their weight. It's rich in potassium, magnesium and iron, while lacking in sodium, fat and cholesterol. And its seeds have even been used in the treatment of certain illnesses.

"It" is the pumpkin. The earliest colonists in America learned about the pumpkin's bounty from Native Americans. When the harvest was good, pumpkins were boiled, baked, dried, smoked, preserved, pickled, and made into jellies, jams, preserves, relishes and condiments.

Best known today as the filling for holiday pies and as the source of festive jack-o'-lanterns, the pumpkin was even used in giving haircuts in the early days of our country. The hard shell of the pumpkin formed the round edge against which hair was cut.

Nature is indeed bountiful. Show your gratitude to God through good stewardship.

They shall come and sing aloud on the height of Zion, and they shall be radiant over the goodness of the Lord. (Jeremiah 31:12)

We give You thanks, Creator, for our abundant blessings.

Name That Saint

The Catholic Church recognizes people who spend their lives serving God and His children with extraordinary faith, hope and love as saints. Some, such as St. Patrick or St. Francis of Assisi, are well-known. Others, less so. Which of these saints are familiar to you?

This saint, known for intense self-discipline and efforts to reform the Church in the 16th century, is the patron saint of night watchmen. (St. Peter of Alcántara)

This saint helped St. Boniface's missionary work in Germany in the 8th century, and was known for humility and kindness. (St. Thecla of Kitzingen)

This saint was the first saint from the Philippines. He endured severe torture and martyrdom for his faith in 17th century Japan. (St. Lorenzo Ruiz)

Whether we become canonized or not, each of us has the opportunity to use our God-given abilities to serve His people.

For you are a people holy to the Lord your God. (Deuteronomy 7:6)

Lord, help me look to the saints as examples for living.

The Biggest Hole in the World

Will you leave a hole in the world?

Eda LeShan, a well-know psychologist, discussed the various aspects of life's journey—including its ending, in her book *On Living Your Life*. She wrote, "It is one of the great miracles of the human experience that each of us is so unique, so special, that we leave a hole in the world when we die. Or do we?

"In facing the inevitability of our own mortality, it seems to me that we need to focus our attention on leaving the biggest hole in the world we possibly can when we are gone, for when we do this, we will stop being afraid. Our attention will be on living, and dying will take care of itself."

That's wise advice. Through your relationships, your work, your whole self, celebrate God's blessings of life and love.

Remove the yoke...the pointing of the finger, the speaking of evil...offer your food to the hungry and satisfy the needs of the afflicted. (Isaiah 58:9,19)

Father, may I use the life You've given me well and bear Your love to all I meet.

Homeowner Help for Financially Distressed

The welcome sign to the Lao Family Community Development center in Oakland, California, gives a sense of the center's inclusive approach: it's printed in eight languages.

Originally established in 1981 to assist war refugees from Southeast Asia, the center has morphed into a haven for crime victims and families in need of financial counseling and income-tax preparation. It also serves as a center to assist in job searches and ways to avoid mortgage foreclosures.

Chery Cheung, one of the center's housing counselors, speaks four languages, which enables her to conduct classes on home buying and money management in clients' first languages—a distinct advantage. Cheung says of the center's clients, "They are so thankful."

How can you help a new citizen become acclimated to a new way of life?

For the Lord your God is bringing you into a good land, a land with flowing streams. (Deuteronomy 8:7)

Make us one in Your goodness, Great Creator.

Making Peace with November

For many, November signals leafless trees, gray skies and an imminent winter of cold winds and snow.

Indeed, this month can be among the dreariest of periods: birds wing south; days shorten and natural light becomes scarce, lending to a generally depressive backdrop for our lives.

From another perspective, however, November can be a time of community. Family and friends, driven indoors by chilly winds and the arrival of winter, can "light lamps, gather around a fire, prepare extra-hearty meals and share hospitality more freely," says Peter Mazar, writing in *Catholic Digest.*

Look to November as a time to reconnect with loved ones and generate warmth through community, love, and generosity. You'll be surprised at how bright the days begin to look.

The dawn from on high will break upon us... who sit in darkness and in the shadow of death. (Luke 1:78-79)

Eternal Father, remind us of Jesus, the Light of the World You sent to abide with us.

The Power of Song

The 2010 earthquake in Haiti was the biggest natural disaster there in 200 years. Thousands upon thousands died and many more were left homeless.

Yet, according to an Associated Press report, "Thousands gathered in public squares to sing hymns." Despite the devastation that surrounded them, a number of Haitians dealt with their emotional pain through the power of prayer—and song.

And many experts agree on the potency of singing. It releases endorphins that relieve pain and reduce stress, and has even been used as a relaxation therapy to help cope with depression, anxiety and other mental health issues.

While we remember the people of Haiti with our prayers and charitable giving, let's try to imitate them by singing even in the midst of our own problems. Think of the words attributed to St. Augustine: "He who sings, prays twice."

O give thanks to the Lord, call on His name. ...Sing to Him, sing praises to Him. (1 Chronicles 16:8-9)

God, grant us inner strength to help us see through difficult times.

When Counting Sheep Won't Cut It

There's probably nothing as frustrating as a sleepless night. Oddly, sometimes the more tired and worn down we are, the harder it is to drift off. Try these tips the next time restful sleep eludes you:

- Enjoy the morning sun: It helps your body rhythms if you soak up sunshine early in the day.
- Exercise early in the evening: Research shows that exercising between 5p.m. and 7p.m. may contribute to a restful sleep.
- Dim the lights: Your body wants to sleep when it's dark.
- Cover your alarm clock: Its bright beams—as well as the sight of time creeping along—can create anxiety.
- Scent your pillow: Lavender can induce relaxation.

And one last thought: maybe it wouldn't hurt to count your blessings and say a prayer or two, either.

I lie down and sleep...for the Lord sustains me. (Psalm 3:5)

Calm us, Redeemer, so we may rest in Your presence.

An Unlikely Heroine

In 1909, Susan Travers was born into privilege. The daughter of a British Royal Navy admiral, her youth was filled with tennis lessons and socializing among the wealthy.

Yet Travers was among the thousands of women who joined the French Red Cross at the outbreak of World War II. Trained as a nurse, Travers instead opted for the more exciting role of ambulance driver. She joined the French expeditionary force to Finland to help in the Winter War against Russia. She later assisted the French Foreign Legion in Africa, then served in Italy and Germany.

Throughout her service, Travers reportedly exhibited nerves of steel, and was said to have shown emotion publicly only once, when the Legion bestowed upon her its *Medaille Militaire*. She was the only woman ever so honored.

Appearances can indeed be deceiving. Try to avoid snap judgments of others.

You shall not render an unjust judgment...with justice you shall judge your neighbor. (Leviticus 19:15)

Jesus Christ, instill in me an open mind free of prejudice.

Mobilizing Youth

Maya Enista is the CEO of Mobilize.org, a website that promotes greater political and civic participation among youth. In her late 20s, she already has eight years of experience working with nonprofit organizations. Her involvement began as a Rutgers University student when she joined MTV's Rock the Vote campaign. Afterwards, she worked with the Hip Hop Civic Engagement Project which encourages political involvement.

Mobilize.org encourages political engagement by youth of all races, classes, faiths and parties. Today's young people "are a much more collaborative and innovative generation," says Enista, and this gives her hope that they can cooperate for social justice.

Participate in government. Vote. Join local or national campaigns that matter to you.

To each is given the manifestation of the Spirit for the common good. (1 Corinthians 12:7)

Help youth especially to be involved in political and civic affairs, Holy Wisdom.

Ring, Relax and Wait

There are 60,000 elevators in residential and commercial buildings across New York City. While most of these rides are uneventful, some end tragically. Five-year-old Jacob Neuman, for example, died while trying to escape from a stalled elevator.

Thus every November, city inspectors teach elevator safety classes to thousands of New York City schoolchildren. They learn a useful saying for anyone who uses elevators: "Ring, relax, and wait." It's a reminder to ring the alarm and wait for help if ever stuck in an elevator.

Robert D. LiMandri, the city's buildings commissioner, hopes that the new mantra will become as widely known as the "stop, drop and roll" fire safety technique.

Issues such as elevator safety may seem trivial, but the simplest advice may save your life or a loved one's.

For Your name's sake, O Lord, preserve my life. (Psalm 143:11)

Keep me and my loved ones safe, Author of life.

Man's Best Friend

Returning veterans must endure the physical and psychological effects of war. Medicine eases the pain, as do trained service dogs. The Veterans Administration has joined with the non-profit Freedom Service Dogs to help soldiers in rehabilitation.

The dogs are rescued from animal shelters and trained for nearly a year. Then, the program pairs them with veterans in Colorado's Wounded Warrior Battalion. The dogs, trained as physical and mental assistants for their disabled owners, provide comfort, love and support. Says Gulf War veteran David Watson of his dog, "We just keep helping each other out."

Diane Vertovec of Freedom Service Dogs believes dogs help soldiers "overcome a lot of their mental instability."

Welcome the healing power of an animal's companionship.

(Tobias)...the angel...and the dog...journeyed along. (Tobit 6:1,2)

Alert us to the healing power of companion animals, Holy God.

The Eleventh Hour of the Eleventh Day...

...of the eleventh month of 1918, that is, 11 a.m. on November 11, 1918, an armistice ended "the war to end all wars."

The Treaty of Versailles was signed in 1919. In that same year, President Wilson proclaimed November 11 as Armistice Day, a day for parades, public meetings and an 11 a.m. suspension of business in honor of veterans. It became a legal holiday in 1938.

By 1954, Armistice Day had become Veterans Day to recognize veterans of World War II and Korea in addition to World War I.

Despite attempts to move it, Veterans Day continues to be observed on the eleventh day of the eleventh month in honor of that first Armistice Day and in tribute to all U.S. veterans of every war.

How can you honor veterans? Start by being an educated, informed and active citizen.

Pay...honor to whom honor is due.
(Romans 13:7)

Gracious Father, thank You for the freedoms we enjoy.

Franciscans for Fair Trade

Fair trade ensures that small farmers and craftspeople from developing countries can compete in the global marketplace while profiting from fair prices.

Franciscan sisters in Pittsburgh, Pennsylvania, have launched a private-label coffee brand called Franciscan Blend, which uses fair-trade beans from Honduras. Income from the sale of this coffee also provides aid for elderly and ill sisters.

And the Honduran coffee farmers benefit from the fair trade practices, receiving stable, fair earnings for their products. Sister J. Lora Dambroski, U.S. provincial for the Sisters of St. Francis of the Providence of God, says, "We feel it's a win-win situation by marketing Franciscan Blend Coffee."

Help support small farmers and craftspeople worldwide. Buy fair trade products and shop at farmers and crafts markets.

It is the farmer who does the work who ought to have the first share of the crops. (2 Timothy 2:6)

Remind us to support small farmers and craftspeople, Jesus, carpenter of Nazareth.

The Struggle To Keep Warm

In many communities, particularly in the Northeast and Midwest, winter weather is more than an inconvenience for older adults on fixed incomes. Low temperatures and high heating costs are a dangerous combination and a cause for concern.

As the *AARP Bulletin* points out, keeping warm is increasingly expensive and people such as Dorothy Conley are hit the hardest. The 81-year-old Massachusetts resident copes with cold by using "lots of blankets and more long underwear!" She also gets assistance with heating charges from government and nonprofit programs.

AARP offers some cost-cutting tips: lower the thermostat and the water heater; replace or clean furnace filters; check for and correct drafts; and, of course, bundle up.

Stay aware of elderly family, friends and neighbors who might need extra help to keep warm this winter.

You have fixed all the bounds of the earth; You made summer and winter. (Psalm 74:17)

Remind me to care for those who do not always have the means to care for themselves, Christ, my Lord.

Things We Say

"I'm so bundled up!" shouted little Ruby as she ran down the street near her home, her mother close behind. Ruby had taken to heart her mother's reminder to bundle up, while reminding passers-by that everything we say, especially to children, has great power.

One website, KidsGoals.com, in writing about "positive parenting," suggests replacing negative words with gentler alternatives. Instead of saying, "I hate when you pick on your sister," parents might try, "I know you can do better because you usually get along so well."

Even when speaking of our own feelings, the accent should be positive, the website continues, and praise, when warranted, should be delivered warmly.

Good feelings and encouraging words are contagious—and can inspire both young and old!

In everyway you have been enriched in Him, in speech and knowledge of every kind. (1 Corinthians 1:5)

Guide my thoughts, Master. May my words speak of Your love.

Cut It Out

Women who are abuse victims often feel powerless to tell their partners to stop. But they can usually talk to their hairdressers.

"The salon may be one of the few places women might be without their abuser around," said attorney Laurie Magid. "You don't have a case unless you have a crime reported in the first place and that is the difficult area of domestic violence."

Cut It Out, started in Alabama, but now a national organization, builds on the existing bond between women and their hairdressers. Salon professionals learn the signs of abuse and how to refer clients to helpful resources, such as local family agencies. More than that, volunteers spread the word in the community that domestic abuse is unacceptable on any level.

Do what you can in your neighborhood by supporting housing and other resources for victims of abuse.

Be wise in what is good and guileless in what is evil. (Romans 16:19)

Show me how to prudently counsel those in need of help, Holy Trinity.

Theater District Gem

In the midst of New York's Theater District is what's been called "a little jewel box of a church." St. Malachy's, also known as the Actors' Chapel, caters not only to tourists, but also to actors, playwrights, directors, dancers, stagehands and others in the theatrical community.

"There aren't many churches in Christendom where the person sitting next to you is likely to be a star of stage, screen or television," writes Angelo Stagnaro in the *National Catholic Register.*

Over the years those stars have included Douglas Fairbanks, George M. Cohan, Don Ameche, Spencer Tracy, Rosalind Russell, Florence Henderson and Bob and Dolores Hope.

Founded in 1902, the church accommodates the needs of its congregants. For instance, an 11 p.m. Saturday Mass was introduced because of the theater's demanding weekend schedules. Every community is unique. Support your own, even as you enjoy and respect others.

In the midst of the congregation I will praise you. (Hebrews 2:12)

Eternal God, assist me in recognizing the needs of my community and in doing my part to improve it.

Back In the Workforce

Change for one person affects the whole family.

When college-educated women return to paid employment after years raising children, they face a period of readjustment at work and at home. So do their spouses and children, notes Sue Shellenbarger in the *Wall Street Journal*.

Although most women were happy to be back at work, things had changed during their absence. One mother needed a crash course in Excel spreadsheets from her 12-year-old daughter.

Returnees often take a cut in pay and status. And they can feel a need to prove themselves again. "They must simultaneously renegotiate their relationships at home, with spouses and kids," says one expert.

One woman said "there can be some tension in the marriage over who does what." Another worried about the effect on her children.

What seems to work best is an understanding that family members pitch in to help each other when change is necessary.

I will be the God of all the families of Israel, and they shall be My people. (Jeremiah 31:1)

Gracious Father, encourage our thoughtfulness in word and deed for those closest to us.

Healthful TV Habits

Most of us would agree that plopping down in front of the television set can be one way to relax after a tough day.

Problem is, numerous studies have suggested that television—in large doses—can actually be bad for your health.

A Mayo Clinic study shows that people who watched TV two hours a day had higher obesity rates than those who sat doing something else, such as sewing, reading or writing. Why?

Fact is, merely sitting and watching TV burns little or no calories. Then, there's the snack factor: People tend to eat while watching television, and studies show that the food TV-watchers choose tends to be high-calorie, high-fat snacks.

Limit your time in front of the set. Be alert to the influence of food advertisements and the risk of overeating or eating unhealthy foods.

Food will not bring us close to God.
(1 Corinthians 8:8)

Teach me to respect my body, my being, Savior Jesus.

It's All Relative

If CNN news anchor Soledad O'Brien knows the meaning of gratitude, it's because she has an uncanny knack for putting life's challenges into perspective.

O'Brien's career is demanding and filled with global travel, yet she doesn't lament her responsibilities. "It's hard to have self-pity about flying a lot when someone else lost their home to a natural disaster," she says.

Moreover, O'Brien forfeits housework and other minutiae to focus on her children. "I come home to a not-so-clean house, but my children are healthy, thank God," she says.

O'Brien's recipe for happiness is simple: rather than squeezing in tons of activities, she says, "Focus on the things that matter—loved ones and spending time with them."

When life's challenges mount, focus on your blessings. They might put your problems in perspective.

Offer to God a sacrifice of thanksgiving. (Psalm 50:14)

Holy Spirit, help me learn what really matters.

A Thanksgiving Present

Greg Horoski, an on-line seller of collectible dolls, and his wife, Diane Yano-Horoski, a college professor, had satisfied their first mortgage, supported his business and paid for his health care with a bank loan.

The loan was sold to another bank, the interest went skyward and his on-going medical bills increased. They paid the exorbitant interest and asked for a restructuring: they owed $291,000 plus $235,000 interest. Then the bank began foreclosure proceedings and the Horoskis got a settlement conference.

Judge Jeffrey Spinner found that the couple's bank had accepted over $800 million in federal bailout money and was also trying to foreclose on an 89-year-old California woman in similar circumstances. He gave the Horoskis a Thanksgiving present: their home, debt free, the loan cancelled. And he censured the bank.

Seek justice and mercy in all your actions.

Speak out for...the right of all the destitute. (Proverbs 31:8-9)

Give us courageous judges who will stand up to the unjust and greedy, God our justice.

Creating Family

It was getting near Thanksgiving, but Sam and Maggie couldn't shake their blues.

For the first time, none of their children, all adults now, would be with them for the holiday. Two were living too far away; the oldest had a commitment with his in-laws.

In the week before Thanksgiving, Maggie discovered friends who would also be solo this year, or who, just being two, didn't want to prepare a feast. Maggie invited them to her house. Each person or couple volunteered to bring a traditional Thanksgiving dish or a dessert. In the end, they were ten neighbors around the table, sharing food and friendship.

We're all God's family, called to be there for one another every day of every year.

All the families of the earth shall be blessed. (Genesis 12:3)

Spirit of Love, we give thanks to You, for You give us all good things.

Letters to Jackie

In the first two months after the death of her husband, President John F. Kennedy, his widow Jacqueline received more than 800,000 condolence letters, telegrams and cards.

The messages of grief included one from Ellen Fitzpatrick, an 11-year-old sixth-grader in Massachusetts on November 22, 1963, the day of the president's assassination. "It made me realize how quickly an event can change everything," she recalled.

As an adult, Fitzpatrick decided to revisit that moment, traveling to the Kennedy Library in Boston and reading through 15,000 of those letters which had been saved. She chose 250 to feature in a book, *Letters to Jackie*.

The project renewed her, Fitzpatrick said. "It makes you see what drives a democracy: the people," she observed.

Reaching out to others in need is our calling as members of God's one family.

Blessed are those who mourn, for they will be comforted. (Matthew 5:4)

Comfort me in my sorrow, Lord. Hear my cry for help.

A Very Right "Wrong" Number

It was 5 a.m. on the day before Thanksgiving. Virginia Saenz picked up her ringing phone, and heard a desperate voice. The caller was Lucy Crutchfield, who was trying to reach her own daughter, but had called the wrong number—Saenz's.

Before the caller realized her mistake, Saenz heard a desperate message: Crutchfield was calling to tell her daughter that she could send her money for food, but it would mean she'd have to miss her own mortgage payment to do it.

"It broke my heart," says Saenz.

Saenz saw only one course of action. She told Crutchfield not to worry, and that she would take care of the food for Crutchfield's daughter. The next day, Saenz sent the young woman and her family enough groceries to last a month.

There's nothing more rewarding than acts of kindness. Spread cheer by exercising a generous heart.

Owe no one anything, except to love one another; for the one who loves another has fulfilled the law. (Romans 13:8)

Warm us with Your limitless love, Holy Spirit.

Bringing Good Works to the Airwaves

FM-Radio DJs Lori and Joshua B can be heard most mornings on Star 105.7 FM in Binghamton, New York, doing their morning show. Come Thanksgiving season, however, the two radio personalities promote more than popular tunes.

Each year, the two spend a full week in a camper in a shopping center parking lot where they accept donations of food for the "Thanks 4 Giving" Food Drive. The effort channels food to Catholic Charities so hundreds of needy families can have a traditional Thanksgiving dinner.

The DJs are always amazed at the outpouring of contributions. One year the drive brought in over 1,900 turkeys, either through cash donations or turkeys themselves. "We remind everyone to give only what they can—even a dollar bill helps," says Lori.

Any act of kindness, however small, makes a difference.

I act with steadfast love, justice, and righteousness in the earth, for in these things I delight, says the Lord. (Jeremiah 9:24)

God of life and love, flourish within us.

Listen Up!

The day after Thanksgiving Day is more than a day to start shopping for Christmas, it's also the National Day of Listening, an event started by StoryCorps, a non-profit organization that documents the lives of ordinary Americans. It's designed to celebrate listening—and talking.

The organization suggests that people spend the day sharing remembrances and, if possible, recording the life stories of loved ones. In fact, StoryCorps offers an online questionnaire to help get conversations started, suggesting topics ranging from the specific (one's happiest moments) to the general (perspectives on life, work, or child-rearing, for example).

StoryCorps encourages people to give a listening ear to a loved one to pay homage to each individual's unique life experience. How can you practice this principle year-round?

Guard your steps when you go to the house of God; to draw near to listen is better than the sacrifice offered by fools. (Ecclesiastes 5:1)

Divine Lord, remind me to listen and to speak with the same courtesy I want others to give to me.

A Person — and Priest — of Significance

Speaking about Father Augustine Tolton, the one-time slave and first black Catholic priest in the U.S., Bishop Wilton Gregory said, "He lived at a time when to be a person of color automatically meant that you were not a person of significance."

Born in Missouri, Tolton's father died while serving in the Union Army; he, his mother and his siblings escaped to Illinois. Priests and nuns taught him to read and write. Barred from U.S. seminaries, he studied and was ordained in Rome in 1886.

By 1891 he had established St. Monica's Church in Chicago, designed and built by blacks for black Catholics. His mother and sister kept house for him. Father Tolton's parishioners appreciated having a pastor they could look up to and respect.

Father Tolton worked for a future where every person would be a person of significance. How can you hasten that day?

You need endurance, so that...you may receive what was promised. (Hebrews 10:36)

Good Shepherd, remind us to judge people by their character, not the color of their skin, for we are equal in Your eyes.

Wheels for Change

At 15, Canadian Rick Hansen sustained a spinal cord injury in a car crash and found himself paralyzed from the waist down.

But that didn't keep him from his passion—sports. In fact, Hansen has won some 20 international wheelchair marathons, including six medals as a Paralympian.

In 1985, Hansen made a journey for others—wheeling some 25,000 miles through 34 countries and raising $26 million for spinal cord injury research and quality of life programs. More importantly, Hansen's Man in Motion World Tour raised the awareness of many, helping them to see the potential of all persons once barriers are removed. His foundation raised an additional $200 million over the next twenty-five years to improve the lives of those with spinal cord injuries.

In our own lives, we should strive to get rid of obstacles that hamper the dignity and advancement of ourselves and others.

Honor everyone. (1 Peter 2:17)

I lift my eyes to You, Sacred Heart. Raise me up.

The Gift of a Scrubbed Floor

Eileen Graham didn't know how she was going to do it all.

Her husband, a Navy commander, was deployed, and she faced a move from Virginia to Rhode Island alone with their two young children. There were boxes to pack and cleaning to finish. By late afternoon, as she left to pick up her car from an oil change, she was exhausted. How would she ever scrub the floors—a must-do task—before she left.

When Graham returned with her car, she found her neighbor Lisa, another navy wife, on her hands and knees, scrubbing the kitchen floor.

"I started crying," she recalled. "It was one of the nicest things anyone ever did for me."

Often it's the small gesture—the smile, the hug, the helping hand—that makes the biggest difference in someone's day.

Let us continually offer a sacrifice of praise to God, that is, the fruit of lips that confess His name. Do not neglect to do good and to share what you have, for such sacrifices are pleasing to God. (Hebrews 13:15-16)

In every moment, I seek Your face, Lord. May I reveal Your kindness always.

Apples and Oranges

The comparison rattled Claire. Imagine being told she was in any way like Mary, a co-worker whose self-important attitude made her hard to be around, let alone to like! It was like comparing an apple to an orange—simply ridiculous, Claire thought.

Yet, Claire found herself listening harder as a colleague continued to speak about Mary. He described her as full of life and filled with great passion for her work; he called her creative and cited several examples.

His words caused Claire to think—and to acknowledge Mary's good qualities and her talents. In fact, Claire started making her own list of pluses about Mary.

All of us in this human family share the same God-spark of goodness and light from our Creator. It's something to remember.

Prudence will watch over you; and understanding will guard you. (Proverbs 2:11)

Bless me with patience and understanding, Holy Spirit.

Building a Chain of Prayer

Some childhood memories can be transformed into even better traditions. Cheryl Lagler of Zionsville, Pennsylvania, for example, wrote in *Guideposts* magazine that she and her family have turned a simple decoration into a way to pray together and to think about others.

"Every year, we jot down the names of loved ones or concerns on red and green strips of paper that we then make into a chain," she said. "Starting December 1, we tear off a link and pray for whoever or whatever is written. It's a great way to remember to pray for those individuals and situations we might otherwise overlook," Lagler continues. "And it's exciting to see the chain grow shorter and shorter as Christmas grows near."

Advent is a time to remember those around us and around the world as we anticipate celebrating the birth of Jesus.

(Jesus) would withdraw to...pray. (Luke 5:16)

Infant of Bethlehem, show me Your adorable face in each person I meet.

The "Quiet" Disease?

In the 1980s, controversy, discourse and awareness of AIDS were on the rise, as the number of cases grew steadily throughout that turbulent decade.

Thirty years later, AIDS still affects people in all walks of life. Yet it's no longer news. AIDS has become a fact of life. The truth is, AIDS continues to ravage families in America and around the world, just as it did when it was first discovered. According to the Centers for Disease Control in Atlanta, as of 2009, AIDS has infected over one million Americans.

Support local and national research into its causes and cures as well as organizations that assist people with AIDS. Help and comfort all people with serious diseases as well as their loved ones.

Lord, have mercy on my son. (Matthew 17:15)

Heal those in trouble, in need or in pain, Good Shepherd.

A Life Lost, A Life Found

The story of martyr Jean Donovan inspired Victoria Cavanaugh to pursue a journey of service and hope through missionary work.

When Cavanaugh was in junior high, she saw a documentary about Donovan, a Maryknoll lay missionary who was murdered along with three nuns in El Salvador in 1980. She was so moved that, as a college student, Cavanaugh determined to travel to El Salvador to help the needy there, especially children, much in the way Donovan did.

She now works alongside orphans, providing them with education, resources and, perhaps most importantly, optimism for their future.

Who inspires courage in you?

She opens her hands to the poor, and reaches out her hands to the needy....She opens her mouth with wisdom, and the teaching of kindness is on her tongue. (Proverbs 31:20,26)

Bless those who labor for the needy in every corner of the earth, merciful Father.

Try A Little Kindness

Imagine these pleasant scenes: a passer-by drops a coin in your parking meter. A shop owner graciously lets you pay next week when you forget your wallet. Strangers smile at you; hold doors open; give you right of way when you are driving.

Rev. Rick Potts writes in *Liguorian* magazine about the value of generosity, kindness and common courtesy: "Hostility and division are everywhere. In the confessional, I hear about sins of impatience and anger more and more frequently. All over, people are quick to lose their tempers and snap at one another. We judge and condemn each other without even wanting to know all the circumstances."

But Rev. Potts doesn't believe all graciousness has disappeared. On the contrary, treating others kindly brightens everyone's day—and outlook on life.

Try a little kindness each day.

You have shown me great kindness. (Genesis 19:19)

Holy Spirit, inspire me to extend myself to others through compassion, consideration and courtesy.

About Odetta

With her deep, clear voice, singer Odetta blended the haunting melodies of American folk music with the compelling messages of the civil rights movement. Her unmistakable and emotive voice was often heard accompanying the black-and-white television images of the freedom marchers and the August, 1963, march on Washington.

Odetta Holmes, who died in 2008, was born in Birmingham, Alabama, during the Great Depression. The songs of prison chain gangs and the chanting of field workers shaped her singing, although she earned a degree in classical music and musical theater from Los Angeles City College. She began singing in coffeehouses, and eventually performed at New York's Carnegie Hall.

One critic called her "a majestic figure in American music, a direct gateway to bygone generations that feel so foreign today."

Experience, education and relationships help make us who we are. What is the shape of your life?

My tongue will sing of Your promise, for your commandments are right. (Psalm 119:172)

Help me appreciate each moment of life, Eternal God.

Growing Hunger, Shrinking Food

2009 was a bad year for hungry people: their number rose to over a billion. According to the United Nations Food and Agriculture Organization, nearly one in seven people on earth are hungry and unable to get the food they need.

The global recession contributed to the problem, but there were other factors: difficult growing conditions in many areas; use of land for bio-fuel crops; varying opinions about pesticides, fertilizers and genetically modified seeds; global warming.

Many nations have pledged money, but a clear-cut plan to deal with hunger is missing. Most agronomists and development experts believe that more food *can* be grown, but doubt that it will happen because of lack of cooperation.

Will you feed the hungry today? Will you urge government leaders to do their part for tomorrow?

Come...blessed by My Father... for I was hungry and you gave Me food...thirsty and you gave Me...drink. (Matthew 25:34,35)

Remind me, Sacred Heart, that You count on me to care for my neighbor in need—down the block or across the ocean.

The Accidental Santa

Cliff Snider didn't just want to don a Santa Claus suit at Christmas—he wanted to be a *great* Santa.

Snider's first gig playing Santa Claus came about when he was just 15 and grieving the loss of his dad who had been killed in a car crash. His youth group leader approached him and said, "Cliff, we've got a special job for you." Although he felt detached from the festivities after his tragic loss, Snider gave it a try.

Now, years later, Snider is a veritable expert Santa Claus. He has attended the Charles W. Howard Santa Claus School in Michigan, and continues to perfect his craft. Most of all, he prays for each and every child who waits in line to see "Santa."

Life is a series of unexpected twists and turns. How we deal with those changes says a lot about who we are.

God is our refuge and strength, a very present help in trouble. (Psalm 46:1)

Redeemer, help me to be brave and to take risks in order to do good.

More Than a Bookworm

The stereotypical librarian of times past is often depicted as a nerdy, shy bookworm, immersed in prose and poetry and hardly at the forefront of communications. Now, that old-fashioned viewpoint has shattered. Today's typical librarian is also a "cybrarian," up-to-speed on the latest online research technologies and the newest sources to access information.

Marilyn Johnson of Westminster, Maryland, an avid library user, has profound respect for her local librarians. Librarians, says Johnson, "are smart, funny and they totally get it." What's more, says Johnson, "we need librarians now more than ever."

With a shrinking household budget plaguing so many, the town library has taken a central role in many people's lives, as buying books becomes more difficult.

A career once viewed as conventional, even prudish, has now become cool and cutting edge. Times change and so can we.

Every matter has its time and way. (Ecclesiastes 8:6)

Steer me from stereotypes and snap judgments, Lord Jesus.

Joyful Sister Thea Bowman

"It's a day-by-day decision that I want to live joyfully. I want to be Good News to other people. And so I try to smile."

Those words from Sister Thea Bowman capture the philosophy of the late Franciscan Sister of Perpetual Adoration who died at 52 from cancer. Once a vibrant, active person, she eventually needed a wheelchair as the disease took hold.

Sister Charlene Smith, co-author of *Thea's Song*, says that "talk of sainthood hovers around her name." The two came from different cultures: Bowman, the great-granddaughter of slaves, was from Mississippi; Smith came from small-town Iowa and says that Bowman changed her outlook "from provincial to universal."

Sister Thea Bowman became "a scholar of distinction, a wise mentor, an acclaimed singer, a spellbinding international speaker, a mystic, a prophet." She was, above all, a woman who wanted other people to remember how much she cared about them.

May the God of hope fill you with all joy and peace in believing, so that you may abound in hope by the power of the Holy Spirit. (Romans 15:13)

Open my heart to joy, God, my God.

No Magic Needed Here

Most parents want only the best for their youngsters. Unfortunately, some families are so dysfunctional that children can suffer from serious, even life-threatening problems.

For instance, in Britain, some teens become "throwaways" and face homelessness. Yet, there's hope for these vulnerable young people. Centrepoint, a center for homeless adolescents, has provided more than 70,000 young people with housing, health care and education since its doors opened back in 1969.

To raise money for the operation, Centrepoint hosts "Sleep Out," an annual event when participant-volunteers spend a night on the streets, experiencing the hardship so many British teens face, while gathering pledges from supporters.

Every community has its own share of problems to confront. Don't be afraid to acknowledge your neighbors' difficulties and to lend a hand to help them.

Religion that is pure and undefiled before God, the Father, is this: to care for orphans and widows in their distress, and to keep oneself unstained by the world. (James 1:27)

Broaden my capacity for compassion, Holy Spirit.

Coping at the Holidays

Holidays can be difficult if you are grieving. While this can mean the death of a loved one, other crises can cause an acute sense of loss. These include: a job lay-off; a serious health diagnosis for you or a family member; the foreclosure of your home; the overseas deployment of a family member—or the return of a wounded loved one. But you can cope.

Limit decorating, cooking and baking. Ask the kids to help. Consider worshipping at a different church or at a different time if there's a low-key service.

Go to a restaurant for the festive meal; or, ask for help preparing one at home. Invite seniors, singles or others who might otherwise be alone to join you.

Above all, make time for rest and reflection—and, possibly, tears—alone or with your family.

Those who mourn...will be comforted. (Matthew 5:4)

God, comfort those who are grieving.

A Sustainable Christmas

Episcopal priest and writer Rev. Barbara Crafton has some suggestions for turning your home into "a living Advent calendar" and letting "Christmas creep into the periphery of our vision."

Rev. Crafton uses a skimpy "volunteer yew" from the backyard for her own family Christmas tree. She suggests using wild greens, prunings and holly sprigs for swags and wreaths to decorate doors and windows.

"I want it all to feel the way it felt when I was a girl, when there wasn't all that much to buy or want," says Rev. Crafton. "It has been a long time since I needed anything I didn't have. I want our Christmas to reflect our intense gratitude. Because it is always those who know very well just how blessed they are who are the greatest blessing to others."

Seek the essence of Christmas in gratitude and simplicity.

Get you up to a high mountain, O Zion, herald of good tidings...say to the cities of Judah, "Here is your God!" (Isaiah 40:9)

Be born anew in us, Promised of Ages!

Stretch Those Pennies

In a tough economy, people need to stretch their money. Mary Hunt advises *Woman's Day* readers to revive some frugal practices from earlier generations:

- Bake bread. Spend about 40 cents for a loaf instead of $4. "I make a big batch of dough on Saturday and pop it into a plastic container in my fridge. Whenever we need bread," writes Hunt, "I pull out dough, let it rest and then bake a loaf, rolls or pizza."

- Use layaway plans. Before credit cards, you could "put an item aside at the store and then make small payments until it was paid in full" without interest. Some stores are again offering it.

- Join a Christmas Club. Popularized during the Great Depression, they allow bank customers to deposit a set amount weekly into a special savings account for withdrawal at year's end.

There are countless good ideas—you just have to think and be creative.

Think over what I say, for the Lord will give you understanding in all things. (2 Timothy 2:7)

Help me use hard times to develop my creativity and clear thinking, Spirit of Counsel.

Don't Give Up Hope

As they struggled one particularly difficult year to make ends meet, Kim and Dale Sheckler nearly gave up hope. Dale's new business was struggling and Christmas was coming. There would be no money to buy gifts for their children.

Even as Kim prayed for personal courage and direction, she tried to lift everyone's spirits by again playing a favorite family movie, *It's a Wonderful Life.*

A holiday classic with James Stewart, the movie is about an honest, generous businessman in despair because of an unexpected financial crisis. By the end, he learns how important his life is and how much he has unknowingly meant to others. He regains hope—as did the Shecklers, whose business eventually became a success.

Don't give up hope. You never know how much your life means to others.

Do not let your hearts be troubled. Believe in God, believe also in Me. (John 14:1)

Holy Redeemer, teach me to love You and Your children and to leave the rest to You.

Joyful Again

Mary Obey remembers the "awful emptiness" following the death of her husband. "I wondered if I was going to feel like that forever," she says. "I felt like part of me had died, too, and there were many times in the next year that I wished I could have."

But then the Illinois native saw a notice in her church bulletin inviting widowed people to a "Joyful Again" program. Obey attended. Her time with others going through similar feelings of pain and loss showed her that her life had changed, but not ended.

"We need to talk about our spouses, so we should let our relatives and friends know this," she explained.

Telling others about our sadness allows them to help us carry our burdens and survive our sufferings. Sharing our joy can help increase the good feelings.

The Lord had anointed me...to comfort all who mourn...to give them a garland instead of ashes, the oil of gladness instead of mourning. (Isaiah 61:1-3)

You are with me in all things, Christ, and I am strong for it.

Crocheted Gifts for Christmas

When southern California was ravaged by wildfires a few years ago, people lost their homes and treasured possessions. That's when a church in San Diego decided to make Christmas a little brighter for those who had lost their holiday ornaments.

People who could crochet were asked to create and donate Christmas tree decorations to replace those burned in the fires. A newsletter from the Crochet Guild of America spread the word and volunteers from around the country supplied colorful crèches, stars, angels and more.

One dedicated volunteer, Marsha Stril of Tacoma, Washington, said, "The ornaments put smiles on the faces of people who needed some good cheer. And when I saw pictures of their decorated trees, it did wonders for my Christmas spirit, too."

Put a smile on the face of someone in need today.

She puts her hands to the distaff and...the spindle. She opens her hand to the poor and...the needy. (Proverbs 31:19-20)

Infant Jesus, help me to open my hand to those who could benefit from the fruits of my talents and labors.

From Homeboys to Dough-boys

As the supervisor of the bakery at Homeboy Industries, Louis Lula Rivera manages the work of 20 employees, making sure ovens, mixing machines and processes are running smoothly.

Rivera feels a unique camaraderie with his team, in that they are all former members of the same East Los Angeles gang, the "East Side 213."

Today, they work alongside each other in a different capacity, "earning an honest living," says Rivera.

The bakery is part of a larger enterprise founded by Father Greg Boyle in L.A. back in 1988, after he grew tired of the violence destroying neighborhoods and lives. One former gang member and bakery employee says, "I've put those days behind me."

A fresh start usually begins with forgiveness. Have you forgiven yourself for your own transgressions?

For if you forgive others their trespasses, your heavenly Father will also forgive you; but if you do not forgive others, neither will your Father forgive your trespasses. (Matthew 6:14-15)

Deepen my ability to forgive others and myself, merciful Savior.

Affording Your Companion Animal

Ollie Davidson, programs manager of Chicago's Tree House Humane Society says, "In times of stress, it's always good to keep people with their pets." The stress of unemployment and home foreclosures means more people cannot properly feed or care for their pets.

Happily some non-profit organizations are helping out. Chicago Tree House has provided feline food assistance and litter for more than 30 years. Demand for dog food more than doubled in 2009. PAWS Chicago began a crisis-care center and food bank as well as a temporary foster care program. Minneapolis' Northeast Community Lutheran Church serves about 300 people monthly. Vaccines and pet food are also available.

What can you do to help your neighbors care for the pets that mean so much to them?

Is not the food cut off before our eyes...How the animals groan! (Joel 1:16,18)

Bless and inspire efforts to keep pets with their humans, especially in times of stress, Creator.

Teaching Witness

The family was gathering for the holidays, and Mary dreaded seeing her sister Jackie. For months now, the two had been estranged. Their last encounter was filled with anger; Jackie's harsh words seemed impossible for Mary to forget.

As the siblings sat at opposite ends of the dining table, Mary listened to the words of the prayer offered before dinner. Her husband Ed spoke of gathering as a family, "bridging distances and differences."

Suddenly Mary rose from her seat and walked to where Jackie was sitting. Mary reached down and embraced her sister, whispering "I love you" into her ear. Jackie replied in kind, the two women welling up with tears.

Mary's youngest daughter watched the events intently, realizing she was seeing reconciliation firsthand.

Often the greatest lessons are the ones our witness teaches.

And forgive us our debts, as we also have forgiven our debtors. (Matthew 6:12)

Help me, Spirit of Love, to bring love and understanding to every moment.

The Difficult, Beautiful Zither

The moment 11-year old Gina Gerbasio saw the alpine zither in her great-grandmother's cluttered attic in New Jersey, she was hooked. It was like no other instrument the child had ever seen, and even a random strum of its many strings emitted a haunting, beautiful sound.

Similar to a harpsichord, the zither probably originated in northern Europe. With its many closely placed strings and wide body, the zither is notoriously difficult to learn.

Gina, who after about a year learned to play a full song on the instrument, studies under William Kolb, one of about 150 trained zither players in the U.S. Both admit that mastering the zither is not easy, but well worth it, because of its beautiful sound.

The most successful people are those who persevere when things are challenging. What helps spur you on?

Happy are those who persevere. (Daniel 12:12)

Strengthen our perseverance, Divine Master.

"Home Plate"

Mary Jo and Gary Kurtz of Massachusetts were going through a rough spot. He had just lost his job; she had had a miscarriage. Trying to sell their house and move to a new city, they were in rented housing. Money was tight. Moreover, each of their families expected them to visit on Christmas Day.

After one upsetting phone call, Mary Jo Kurtz said she wanted "Santa to come down our chimney." More than anything she wished their 4-year-old son could "remember being home for Christmas—our home."

But, according to their story in *Catholic Digest*, the Kurtzes made it through the bad times and learned from them. Today they attend Christmas Eve Mass, then stay in their "jammies" on Christmas. They play their favorite music, eat steak from their best china, look for Santa's surprises all through the house, and call all their relatives.

No matter the holiday, make it your family's celebration.

Give good gifts to your children. (Luke 11:13)

Encourage parents and children to establish their own holiday celebrations, Jesus, child of Mary.

To Save a Life

Michael Stolowitzky was a little boy in Poland when World War II broke out. His father was captured while on a business trip to Paris and never seen again. Michael's mother took her son and Gertruda Bablinska, his nanny, to Lithuania.

Not long afterwards Michael's mother died of a stroke, but Bablinska promised her that she'd raise Michael as her own son. Though she was Catholic, she never let the boy forget his Jewish heritage. She protected him from the violence and danger until the war ended and they were able to emigrate to Israel.

Michael Stolowitzky remembers his nanny with gratitude: "Gertruda saved my life. I will never be able to repay her for what she did but as long as I'm alive, I can tell her story."

May each of us care for those in trouble, whatever the cost.

**Love your neighbor as yourself.
(Matthew 22:39)**

Abba, remind me to open my heart to anyone in need of Your mercy.

A Cathedral Church is Restored

A week before Christmas, 2001, a fire blazed through the Cathedral Church of St. John the Divine in New York. The Romanesque and Gothic structure was grimy with soot from the smoke. The organ with its 8,500 pipes needed cleaning. Two seventeenth century Italian tapestries were seriously damaged. Water from the firefighters' hoses collected on the stone floor.

Sections of the cathedral had to be closed for expensive and difficult reconstruction over the next several years. The organ and tapestries were repaired. The full cathedral was reopened on November 30, 2008, to great joy from the whole congregation.

You may encounter obstacles that seem impossible to overcome. But over time and through perseverance and patience, you can conquer anything.

Bear fruit with patient endurance. (Luke 8:15)

Give us the time, perseverance and patience to face problems, Paraclete. Above all, help us to trust in Your care.

Wonders of the Earth

Since the middle ages, 265 million cubic feet of salt has been extracted from vast chambers stretching 155 miles and reaching a depth of almost 1100 feet beneath Wieliczka, near Cracow, Poland.

There's a long tradition of marking places where miners died with a cross using the rock salt itself. Starting in the early 20th century, beautiful bas-reliefs, statues, altars and whole chapels of salt were sculpted as an expression of faith, most depicting the life of Jesus. And 800,000 visitors tour the amazing salt mine galleries each year.

Since God is everywhere, it should come as no surprise that even in the depths of the earth, the human and the divine meet in beauty and in worship.

Where can I go from Your Spirit? (Psalm 139:7)

God of Loveliness, help us seek Your way and Your will, even in the unlikeliest of circumstances.

Snow Lesson

Ann was in a panic. A major snowstorm threatened the area on the weekend before Christmas. Her husband's small retail business would surely suffer, plus she was swamped by all that remained on her own holiday "to do" list.

As she rushed to catch her train home that Friday night, Ann caught sight of a man playing a keyboard near the holiday shopping booths set up inside New York City's Grand Central Station. Two little girls were laughing and dancing. Nearby, shoppers selected treasures for gift-giving. Still more folks smiled at the beautiful decorations.

Ann recalled her family's fun Christmas visits to the city—and her grandchildren's excitement about the coming snow. Let it snow, she thought, realizing that no matter the weather, she had much to be happy about.

Don't let worries stifle your happiness or steal away life's precious moments.

Do not fear or be dismayed. (Deuteronomy 31:8)

Calm my fears, Lord. Fill my heart always with Your joy.

Not Just Another Novel

Charles Dickens' *A Christmas Carol* is a perennial favorite when it comes to stories and films about Christmas. Its place in pop culture is firmly rooted, especially the book's miserly main character, "Scrooge."

What many may not know about Dickens' famous novel is that the author had much more than money, fame and popularity in mind when he wrote it. Dickens felt a deep sense of responsibility as an artist to make clear to his readers how to lead a moral life. He was intent upon showing, through his work, that Christianity was important in guiding one's beliefs and actions.

Dickens once told a friend: "When I exercise my art, one of my most constant endeavors…is to exhibit the teachings of our great Master (Jesus Christ)."

What spiritual and moral teachings underscore the choices you make at Christmas and every day?

Look, the virgin shall conceive and bear a son, and they shall name Him Emmanuel," which means, "God is with us." (Matthew 1:23)

Teach me to walk the walk of faith, Holy Child of Bethlehem.

Beyond Knowledge to Mercy

In 1931, Winston Churchill, the great British statesman who within a decade would be his nation's prime minister as it contended with the horrors of World War II, wrote these words:

"Certain it is that while men are gathering knowledge and power with ever-increasing and measureless speed, their virtues and their wisdom have not shown any notable improvement.

"It is therefore above all things important that the moral philosophy and spiritual conceptions of men and nations should hold their own amid these formidable scientific evolutions. Without an equal growth of Mercy, Pity, Peace and Love, science herself may destroy all that makes human life majestic and tolerable. There never was a time when the hope of immortality and the disdain of earthly power and achievement were more necessary for the safety of the children of men."

That time is still with us. May mercy, pity, peace and love grow in us for tomorrow's sake.

By this we know that we love the children of God, when we love God and obey His commandments. (1 John 5:2)

Lead us in virtue, Holy Paraclete. May we do Your will.

When Small Can Be Very, Very Big

Success is often measured by magnitude: the executive who makes millions; the retailer that racks up billions in sales. According to popular culture, more is better.

But at Community Women Against Hardship (CWAH), small steps are seen as great leaps toward success. Founded in 1988, CWAH is a volunteer organization dedicated to improving the quality of life for women and children in poverty.

Progress, not perfection or massive change, is considered success. Each move toward self-sufficiency and freedom from drugs or domestic abuse is considered an achievement, and is based on each client's starting point.

"Our clients are often suffering from a poverty of spirit as much as a poverty of possessions," says Gloria Taylor, co-founder of CWAH. "The challenge is changing people's perspectives."

What's your perspective? How do you measure success?

Human success is in the hand of the Lord. (Sirach 10:5)

Let us be encouraged by small achievements, loving Lord.

Help Youngsters Help Themselves

Father Edward Flanagan started Boys Town, in Omaha, Nebraska, in 1917. Today it also accepts girls. Their philosophy is that troubled kids need to learn positive life skills and to develop their spiritual and educational lives.

At the juvenile justice program run by Boys Town in Washington, DC, youths in trouble with the law learn to accept responsibility and to respect themselves and others.

Payton and Yadelska Wynne are family teachers and role models who take youngsters into their home and give them support and structure. The youngsters have a set routine including time for meals, chores, classes, homework, and self-government meetings.

"Since I've been here I've been working on a relationship with my father," said a 16-year-old. "I just didn't respect my father because of his drinking."

Do all you can to help young people in your own town.

The revealed things belong to us and to our children forever. (Deuteronomy 29:29)

Guide Your children, Eternal Father, in growing in wisdom, age and grace.

Noble Steeds, Wonderful Day

Heather Marcus had a special treat in store for her 3-year-old daughter Ella one sunny winter day. They went to a farm in Townshend, Vermont, where owner Robert Labrie introduced them to his magnificent Friesian horses, the stars of the day's outing.

Labrie brought out a red sleigh with two of his horses pulling it. Marcus and her little girl climbed in and sat under a cozy blanket. Then they enjoyed a magical afternoon riding through the snowy countryside, listening to the clop-clop of the horses' hooves and the jingling of the brass bells on their harnesses. Neither wanted the memorable adventure to end.

Find delight in the simplest things. By cherishing the little moments, we are able to find true happiness with our loved ones and God.

Have you not known? Have you not heard? The Lord is the everlasting God, the Creator of the ends of the earth. (Isaiah 40:28)

Lord, thank You for blessing me with little things that can mean great happiness.

Sewn With Love

Sewing is a popular hobby for many. Clare Liptak of New Jersey has found a way to combine her knack for sewing with her faith as a way to help the poor in Africa.

Liptak collects fabric and sewing machines to send to women in Tanzania who sew clothes for themselves and their families. So far, she has shipped approximately 80 machines there, along with fabric, sewing supplies, carpentry tools and other items.

Liptak says the work is not only fun, but also meaningful for both the recipients and donors of the machines. "Many people don't want their grandmother's sewing machine thrown away," she explains. At the same time, they may just be gathering dust from disuse. So she enjoys collecting them and sending them to those who truly need them.

How could your gifts and talents help the needy?

Just as you did it to one of the least of these... members of My family, you did it to Me. (Matthew 25:40)

Remind me, Jesus, that in serving others, I serve You.

Are You In a Rut?

Could this coming year be the one when you shake up your life, get out of a rut and make positive changes?

Although the New Year's holiday is a good time for change, any time of year is fine once you're ready for it. Writing in *Body and Soul*, Cheryl Richardson offers a few ideas to get you started thinking about new possibilities: "Sign up for a public speaking course to finally feel comfortable in front of a crowd; get yourself into therapy to help you quit a self-destructive habit once and for all."

She suggests you think about your life in a new way. For example, imagine a future where you really quit smoking or are no longer afraid to go flying.

After thinking about what you want to change, take some action toward that goal. You might be pleasantly surprised by what you can accomplish.

For I know their works and their thoughts, and I am coming to gather all nations and tongues. (Isaiah 66:18)

Eternal Father, help me to be open to Your desires for me and my true welfare.

Also Available

We hope that you have enjoyed *Three Minutes a Day, Volume 45*. These other Christopher offerings may interest you:

- **News Notes** are published 10 times a year on a variety of topics of current interest. Single copies are free; quantity orders available.

- **Appointment Calendars** are suitable for wall or desk and provide an inspirational message for each day of the year.

- **DVDs** range from wholesome entertainment to serious discussions of family life and current social and spiritual issues.

- **Website — www.christophers.org —** has *Christopher Closeup* radio programs, podcasts of *Christopher Minutes,* as well as uplifting stories, columns and other motivational material

For more information on The Christophers or to receive News Notes or a catalogue of additional material, please contact us:

The Christophers
5 Hanover Square
11th Floor
New York, NY 10004
Phone: 212-759-4050 / 888-298-4050
E-mail: mail@christophers.org
Website: www.christophers.org

The Christophers is a non-profit media organization founded in 1945 by Father James Keller, M.M. We share the message of personal responsibility and service to God and humanity with people of all faiths and no particular faith. Gifts are welcome and tax-deductible. Our legal title for wills is The Christophers, Inc.